FACING FACTS IN
MODERN MISSIONS

FACING FACTS
IN MODERN MISSIONS

A Symposium

MOODY PRESS

CHICAGO

Printed in the United States of America

7614   58

CONTRIBUTORS

Milton Baker, President of Evangelical Foreign Missions Association, Foreign Secretary of Conservative Baptist Foreign Missions Society

Raymond B. Buker, Sr., Conservative Baptist Theological Seminary

Arthur M. Climenhaga, President of Messiah College, Grantham, Pennsylvania

Paul G. Culley, Director of Division of Missions, Columbia Bible College

Melvin L. Hodges, Secretary for Latin America, Assemblies of God

Edwin E. Jacques, Foreign Secretary of Conservative Baptist Foreign Missions Society

Noel Perkin, Executive Secretary Emeritus of Foreign Missions, Assemblies of God

Clyde W. Taylor, Executive Secretary of The Evangelical Foreign Missions Association

Hubert Reynhout, Jr., Barrington College

J. F. Shepherd, Nyack Missionary College

Merrill C. Tenney, Wheaton College

Timothy M. Warner, Fort Wayne Bible College

FOREWORD

Is THE LIBERAL WING of the ecumenical movement justified
in assuming that foreign missions and missionaries in most
of the world are becoming obsolete except as a supplement
to the outreach of the younger churches? Do the terms "ecumenical mission," "fraternal worker," or "church aid" better
conform to scriptural teachings than our usual terms "foreign
missions," "missionaries," and the "indigenous church"? If
the missionary is a "sent one," from whom is he sent and to
whom? Should he be responsible to the younger church on
the field or to the church back home? Should he be a member of the church on the field or retain membership back
home? In the area of financial assistance, what does Scripture indicate as to the channeling of foreign funds to the
younger church for the support of missionaries (fraternal
workers) and for the work of the younger church? In the
light of the Scriptures have we been mistaken in our concept
of the "indigenous church" as being self-governing, self-
supporting, self-educating and self-propagating? Is "church
aid" of the ecumenical mission destructive of the above
principles?

These matters were discussed at meetings of the Evangelical Foreign Missions Association. There was great interest in the issues and this symposium is the result.

The Rev. Noel Perkin, past president of the Evangelical
Foreign Missions Association and retired general secretary
of the Foreign Missions Division of the Assemblies of God,
has served as editor and has written the final chapter of the

symposium. On behalf of our association, we wish to express our sincere appreciation to Mr. Perkin and to all the contributors to this volume for the time and effort taken to make it possible.

CLYDE W. TAYLOR
Executive Secretary
Evangelical Foreign Missions Association

CONTENTS

9

RECOMMENDED READING

BAVINCK, J. H. *An Introduction to the Science of Missions*. Grand Rapids: Baker Book House, 1960.

BROWN, ARTHUR J. *The Foreign Missionary*. New York: Fleming H. Revell, 1907.

FIFE, ERIC S. and GLASSER, ARTHUR F. *Missions in Crisis*. Chicago: Inter-Varsity Press, 1962.

LaMOTT, WILLIS. *Revolution in Missions*. New York: The Macmillan Company, 1954.

McGAVRAN, DONALD A. *How Churches Grow*. New York: Friendship Press, 1960.

WARREN, MAX. "The Meaning of Identification," *The Theology of the Christian Mission*, ed. Gerald H. Anderson. New York: McGraw-Hill Book Company, Inc., 1961. Pp. 229-238.

CHAPTER I

THE MOTIVES AND GOAL
OF WORLD MISSIONS

MOTIVES

Merrill C. Tenney

THE LAST DECADE has brought new developments in the political and religious attitudes of non-Christian nations that have affected seriously the whole enterprise of Christian missions and that may well call for a complete reappraisal of the philosophy of missionary endeavor. The rise of a nationalism that spawned not less than seventeen independent nations on the continent of Africa in 1960, creating such tensions that foreigners were compelled to withdraw from some regions at least temporarily, raised the question whether missionaries could anticipate any permanent stay in these countries. The growth of national churches, independent of the denominational organizations that originally sponsored them, has posed the problem of their relation to the parent bodies as well as the attitude those bodies should hold toward the entire missionary enterprise. If the various "fields" are relegated to the national churches operating with their own funds and personnel, will they be able to maintain the work and will the home churches lose all incentive for missionary effort? Furthermore, the closing of the doors to the vast unevangelized populations of China and Russia,

13

the increasing unwillingness of India to accept foreign preachers, and the pressures of the Roman Church in territory where it is politically dominant have sealed off access to a large proportion of the world's population who would have little opportunity to hear the gospel except through aid from outside.

In addition to the external problems presented by the pagan world in general there is the internal problem of the church itself. The ecumenical movement, striving to achieve organic union among the various denominations, has already begun a different policy toward missions. The opinion that work should be coordinated without regard for doctrinal distinctions, and the attitude that Christianity is not essential to salvation seem to constitute the prevalent mood. Sharing our sentiments with the followers of other faiths rather than proclaiming to them an imperative and saving gospel is recommended in the name of fraternal tolerance.

If policies must be changed to fit these new conditions, on what basis shall the change be made? What shall be the strategy of the evangelical churches in the coming era? Unquestionably many old methods must be discarded, but does the situation demand a drastic alteration of basic principles?

Evangelicals turn to the Bible for the answers to their problems because they recognize that the Scriptures lay down the fundamental program for the operation of the church, even though details of application may vary with time and culture. Many of our problems are not new, though they may appear in a new dress. The world is no more pagan now in proportion to its total population than it was in the first century, when the church was just beginning its work, and when the Book of Acts was written. The power of imperial Rome was as great a threat to the preaching of the gospel as Communism or Islam today. If the church had a successful program then—and it did—its features ought to be applicable to our own time.

Fundamental to the entire missionary enterprise is motive. Why should the church engage in evangelism? If the followers of other religions are convinced that their faith is adequate for their needs and is suited to their culture, why should we disturb them by insisting that they adopt another creed which is adapted to Western mentality and which may be essentially no better than theirs? The tacit assumption that Christianity is merely a religious phase of Western culture lends aid to this type of thinking and tends to paralyze the nerve of missionary endeavor.

I. *Obedience to Christ*

The missionary enterprise is not an annex to Christianity added by enthusiasts with a mania for proselyting; it is an inherent part of the gospel message. The entire career of Christ was missionary in nature, for He came "not to be ministered unto, but to minister, and to give his life a ransom for many" (Mark 10:45). He was the living Word of God who announced to all men the purpose and will of the Father. He was constantly under the compulsion of reaching out to new persons or groups. His final instructions to His disciples demanded that they go into the whole world and preach the gospel to every creature. Any serious attempt to perpetuate His teaching must inevitably involve missionary effort.

Furthermore, the message of Christ is not a native aspect of Western culture. Christianity began in the Middle East, at the border of East and West, and belongs to both. In no sense is it the exclusive property or product of either. The Great Commission recognized no geographical boundaries or preferred spheres of activity. Christ commanded that His Word should be preached to all men.

Obedience to Christ is therefore the prime motive for missions. As the Duke of Wellington said, the Great Commission is the marching orders of the church. To abandon missionary effort would be a betrayal of the entire calling of the Church of God, and a repudiation of the lordship of Christ. If He possessed the authority which He claimed, and if He is still living and supervising His Church, there can be no excuse for abandoning the missionary enterprise. On the contrary, it should be strengthened as the pagan population of the world increases and as opposition becomes more intense.

II. *The Lost State of Man Without Christ*

A necessary corollary of this motive is the recognition of the lost state of men without Christ. Why did Christ come to earth to die if the need were not urgent? Would He have sacrificed His life, and demanded that His followers devote theirs to the proclamation of forgiveness of sins and the establishment of the kingdom of God? A healthy man needs no medicine; a saved world needs no gospel. Paul, in speaking of the inevitable judgment, says, "Knowing therefore the terror of the Lord, we persuade men" (II Cor. 5:11). Recognizing that they were imperiled by their sins, he felt constrained to carry to them the news of salvation.

Certainly this motive is not nearly so potent now as it once was. The study of comparative religions, influenced by an evolutionary philosophy, has fostered the concept that all religions have a common origin in the human attempt to find some external reality that can order the universe and explain its phenomena. Because these faiths arise from human aspirations and desires, they are all equally valid (or invalid), and consequently one can be regarded as superior to the other only insofar as it improves human values. One may be more logical or satisfying than another, but none can claim to be the exclusive way of salvation. As all the spokes of a wheel lead to the hub, the various faiths all lead back to the one God, whether He be called Brahma, Allah, or Jehovah.

The fallacy of this argument is patent to all who have ever made a serious comparison with other theologies. In them there is only a shallow estimate of sin and a very unsatisfactory view of the person of man and of God. Either sin is relatively inconsequential and has little bearing on human destiny, or else God does not demand holiness of His creatures. Diametrically opposing concepts of the being of God, of the nature of man and of sin cannot both be true. If, as the New Testament states, all have sinned and have come under divine condemnation for their acts and nature, they are lost and need the knowledge of the gospel. The reflection of the motive appears clearly in the New Testament. Paul speaks of having the message of reconciliation committed unto him, and of being an ambassador responsible for discharging his commission. Missions, according to the Bible, are not a transient enthusiasm aroused by humanitarian zeal, but are the outcome of a serious realization that men without Christ are without hope and without God in the world.

The motive of charity which sometimes actuates missionary endeavor does not belong to it peculiarly. The desire to aid underdeveloped countries economically and socially has in recent time become the concern of the State, and millions of dollars have been devoted to foreign aid for the purpose of improving the economy of backward peoples. Unquestionably the relief of suffering and aid to the impoverished are normal fruits of Christian love. James asserted that the poor should be fed as an expression of genuine faith in God (James 2:14-16). The early church undertook the responsibility of feeding its own poor and of supporting the widows and the unemployed who were unable to care for themselves. The material effects, however, were never the chief motive but were an important by-product of the greater task of propagating the message of Christ.

An excellent illustration of the cultural by-products of missionary endeavor may be found in the work of the

Wycliffe translators. While their main purpose is to place the dynamic of the Word of God in the hands of people who would not otherwise possess it, they have made a tremendous contribution to literacy, sanitation, agriculture, and other betterments through their own example of self-support. Whole villages and districts have been made clean and prosperous through the effects of the gospel. The church should engage in missions in order to carry out the command and plan of Christ. Education, economic betterment, and moral uplift are inescapable concomitants of salvation and may provide secondary motives for action.

GOAL: DISCIPLESHIP

THE OBJECTIVE of the missionary enterprise is discipleship. The Great Commission as cited by Matthew (28:19-20) lays chief stress upon making disciples of all the nations; the teaching and baptizing are subordinate means employed to produce the end. Discipleship involves the readiness to accept the authority and teaching of Jesus, and to attach oneself to His person as a devout and honest follower. To receive His teaching concerning God, Himself, man, sin, and salvation, to meditate on it and absorb it, and to commit oneself so fully to Christ that He becomes paramount in personal plans and in life is discipleship. Discipleship is the sincere adoption of a master's ethic and teaching, not merely holding an opinion. The full understanding of regeneration and of the subsequent aspects of Christian experience can best be imparted by the creation of disciples.

Discipleship may be a slow process, because it involves growth. Conversion is instant, hinging on the decision to become a disciple; but maturity of experience requires training and time. Large numbers of converts may not always indicate success, nor the lack of them failure. Sometimes a sudden mass response is the result of superficial understanding or of unworthy motives. A few Christians who are certain of their hope, settled in conviction, and ethically sound are worth a hundred who are only nominal in their allegiance to Christ.

Discipleship involves evangelization because as each imparts his knowledge to another and undertakes the responsibility of teaching him, the message is spread from person to person. One sometimes wonders whether the elaborate organization and costly equipment employed in much of our missionary evangelism is necessary. Does the transplanting of Western living conditions to other lands increase the efficiency of missionary endeavor or does it create an obstacle for the gospel? Will missionaries become so engrossed in operating their machinery that they will have no time for the personal contacts that make disciples? One consecrated follower of Christ, soundly converted and thoroughly trained in Christian thinking and ethic, is worth a dozen committees or a loudspeaker system. Mass evangelism is useful and scriptural, but the individual national aflame with the gospel is worth more, for he can reach his own people better than the foreigner, who must overcome the handicaps of the language barrier, cultural differences and political prejudice.

One suggestion emanating from the neo-orthodox theology is that the church includes all mankind, except that the great bulk of humanity is at present "uncommitted." According to the New Testament no man is a Christian until he is "committed"; "as many as received him, to them gave he power to become the sons of God, even to them that believe on his name" (John 1:12). The church does not merely absorb or educate unbelievers. They must declare a committal before they become part of it.

It is, therefore, unsound policy to treat unbelievers as if they were already Christians. Perhaps the term "heathen" could be discarded, since it has acquired the connotation of ignorance and barbarism which will not fit many non-Christian peoples today; nevertheless, the Bible states that man is "dead in trespasses and sin" until he is quickened by God, and there is no logic in pretending that a corpse is alive. Salvation is the impartation of life, not just joining a new society.

Evangelism through discipleship is the most effective approach today. Appeal to the masses directly is impossible in some countries and possibly inadvisable in others, but the impartation of faith by personal testimony is always effective and paves the way for more general methods. A transformed life is the best advertisement for Christ, and the personal explanation of the meaning of salvation in terms of common experience outweighs the formal presentation of doctrine, though the latter may be useful in instructing church groups.

Creating organizations and erecting buildings cannot be the major task of missions. Organization can be promoted purely for its own sake; buildings and property, though often necessary to permanence of the church, can be destroyed or confiscated; but the faith that is engendered in the hearts of believers cannot be dissipated by external pressure. The early Christian churches prior to the age of Constantine had little formal organization; they worshiped in private homes and, when driven underground, in the catacombs; but they maintained such vitality that when they emerged from hiding at the end of the persecutions, they had become the most powerful single influence in the Roman world.

Discipleship means the ultimate transformation of society, for a group of people dedicated to Christ cannot avoid changing the attitudes and practices of the society in which they live. The church's business is creating new lives, not new lobbies. If the church becomes merely one more reform bloc it will inevitably be classed only as a social movement representing a phase of opinion rather than as the people of God empowered by a spiritual dynamic. Christians should affect the social structure in which they live, but nowhere in the Bible are missions equated with social re-

orm apart from the regeneration of the individual. To assert
hat by changing social environment through legislation the
:hurch will accomplish its mission is equivalent to saying
hat it can produce the desired effects without the cause.
Certainly the church as an organization should take its stand
or improvement of education, for moral uplift, and for
)etter economic conditions; but it must never confuse the
)roximate goals of time with the ultimate goals of eternity.
[t must always remember that "the things which are seen
are temporal; but the things which are not seen are eternal"
(II Cor. 4:18).

Missions are not obsolete, although the next decade may
)ring great changes in techniques. The last nineteen cen-
uries have witnessed many profound social and religious
:hanges, but the church has always been a missionary church
wherever it has been truly active. As long as large sections
)f the world live in ignorance of Christ, there will be a need
or preachers and teachers. Missions, however, ought not
:o be one department of church organization, which can be
·elegated to a secondary place or treated as a luxury; they
:hould be an expression of the church's total thrust. The
answer to the present dilemma is not fewer missionaries but
nore who know the Scriptures and who are self-supporting.
These can always gather around themselves small individual
groups for prayer, study, and worship, which can be formed
into active churches. Wherever there is a genuine knowl-
3dge of Christ, it will be communicated; where it is com-
nunicated, it will gather disciples; and where it gathers
disciples, there will be a missionary movement.

MOTIVES

Paul G. Culley

THE WORK OF MISSIONS is the work of Christ. He is per
sonally in action when His missionary, by the moving of the
Holy Spirit, prays and preaches and leads sinners to Him
Christ is expressing His love toward them through His mes
sengers.

A retrospect through the history of missions discloses a
consistent emphasis on this primary relation of the mis
sionary to his Master. Motivation separated from Christ
proves ephemeral and inadequate. As Zinzendorf put it, "I
have one passion; it is He, and He alone."

I. *Primary Motives, Depending on the Love of God*

God's motive is found in His love. "God so loved . .
that he gave" (John 3:16).

The love of God is the one adequate motivation for the
Christian likewise. When the Apostle Paul analyzed his work
as a missionary, he found that "the love of Christ con-
straineth us" (II Cor. 5:14). Any service given outside the
context of God's love carries no message and brings no
reward.

The operation of the love of God is not dependent on the
response of the objects of His love. "While we were yet
sinners, Christ died for us" (Rom. 5:8). The missionary who
goes with such motivation has adequate power for endur-
ance and for completion of the mission on which he is sent.

Missionaries testify to the fact that subordinate considerations were effective in getting them to a field of service
but were inadequate in keeping them there over the long
pull. "Only divine love filling the heart and pervading the
life is equal to the tests and demands of true missionary
service," wrote R. H. Glover.

Personal experience in being related to the love and will of God may express itself in a number of responses:

Devotion to the person of Christ
Gratitude for His benefits
Desire to vindicate Him before mankind and His enemies
Ambition to help complete the Body of Christ
Jealousy for His name
Obedience to His commands
Hunger and thirst for His righteousness
Longing for His return
Love for the brethren
Concern for the salvation of sinners

Any of these can be classified as a primary or godly motive.

The Holy Spirit uses a variety of experiences in awakening the concern of a Christian for those who have never heard the message of the gospel. To see or hear of the unevangelized masses in China and India commonly awakens a sense of their need and of our personal responsibility. To face the reality of demon powers in New Guinea and Africa can be the beginning of a call to personal commitment as a soldier of Jesus Christ. Recognition of a need and ability to meet that need, however, do not necessarily spell out a call of God to that particular service; without the personal call, many have met failure and heartbreak in the face of disillusionment. Raymond W. Frame tells of one young lady who was stirred by a missionary address with pictures of little children, to whom she sensed an immediate call for service. Her love for the people of that land deepened, and she could hardly wait until she had reached them and had learned their language. Then after suffering through indignities and thieveries, her love of the people evaporated, and when the children mocked her and ran from her, she had no more desire to help them. Her human pity was deficient in supplying strength for the task. Only in spiritual revival was supernatural love provided.

II. *Motives Depending on the Enthusiasm of the Missionary*

Secondary motives, good motives, are readily discerned, in addition to the primary motivation that has its source in God Himself, who is love. Each of these is dependent upon personal enthusiasm, an uncertain psychological quality.

1. A natural sense of human sympathy and pity, called out by the presence of suffering, has sent many missionaries to places of need. There is much gratification in the work of treating diseased bodies, and an immediate reward in seeing them become well and strong. Deep poverty stirs many a heart. Even unrepentant sinners may borrow enough altruism to sense a responsibility for the neighbor who is in need. The degraded condition of women, the helpless life of a slave, murder of unwanted children, burial of living survivors—these and other evil practices arouse pity, and have been effective in calling out many missionary volunteers.

2. A stronger call is in the spiritual need of the heathen. Their lost condition is not a fact of secondary importance, but one's response to this fact may be on a secondary level of motivation, through which one is moved with much enthusiam, yet not possessed by the infinite love of Christ.

3. One's duty may seem clear, in obedience to the command of Christ, yet observance of duty as a military response may take one to a mission field and leave him helpless in the frustration of ineffective service. To read a command in the Bible is only the beginning of service. Christ must be personally in control, by the filling of the Holy Spirit.

4. Ambition to see the church planted in every land is indeed a noble sentiment. Enthusiasm for this goal, however, when the lonely missionary is far from encouraging companionship, may wither like a plant in time of drought.

Our Lord recognized this in holding His disciples in Jerusalem until the Holy Spirit was sent, thus energizing them for effective witnessing.

These motives, such as depend upon one's own desire and determination, are fickle. The strong man going in his strength will prove weaker than the one whose weakness is filled with the love of Christ. Christ's love never fails.

III. *Motives Depending on Borrowed Convictions*

Motives of a third group, not bad in themselves, are inferior and deceptive. These involve loyalty, but the springs of life and love have been borrowed from another person.

How many Christian young people have been given to the Lord before they were born! A pious heritage is a great gift, but to go as a missionary because of parental convictions can be an empty gesture.

The desire to please a teacher, pastor, friend, and, still more subtle, the desire to be a representative of the home church on the mission field can be hypocrisy and can feed a selfish pride. Volunteers for missionary service from Bible schools and missionary conferences need particularly to be examined for dependence upon group enthusiasm; such a call might represent little more than conformity to a culture pattern. One missionary wrote home, "Tell the students to dig their own wells before coming away to a foreign land." The supply of grace obtained once a year in a Bible conference, or once a week through a helpful sermon, or carried in treasured notebooks is not sufficient for the daily grind of a tiring and weakening struggle against the forces of darkness. "My grace is sufficient for thee" (II Cor. 12:9). And a continuing experience of our Lord's sufficiency is dependent upon a continuing walk with Him.

IV. *Motives Depending on Natural and Selfish Responses*

A familiar expression in appealing for missionary volunteers has been, "Invest your life where it will count most." There is a good purpose in urging a young person to consider eternal results and the rewards in serving God. Basically, however, this approach is wrong. It assumes that a man has something to give and that his decision will determine how that gift to God is to be made. Scripture teaches that "neither is he that planteth anything, neither he that watereth; but God that giveth the increase" (I Cor. 3:7). When we present our bodies to God, our preferences are eliminated. To determine, therefore, where my life will most profitably be invested neglects to recognize that, apart from God, I am bankrupt, and that my identification with Him in service calls for denial of any right to my goal and my own method and my personal reputation. My relationship to the Lord Jesus Christ is that of a slave to a master. The kingdom of God is an absolute sovereignty.

Worldly standards must be set aside in a supernatural work. God has established Jesus Christ alone as having authority (Matt. 28:18). It is our privilege to know and to do His will. Laws of economics and the best counsel in public relations are not decisive in the work of missions. Principles of psychology and sociology must give way to the law of faith and obedience. It is true that a man may hide a willful and proud disposition under the cloak of a spiritual call, but this danger need not discourage us from expecting God's work to be on the basis of supernatural energy. One benefit of association together in a missionary society is that God's directions to His servants are confirmed through others in the society. When confirmation of personal guidance is lacking, one must distrust the perception of that guidance. A group that is fully agreed on the Lord's will in a matter, having set aside every selfish incentive, may confidently expect God to accomplish what He has revealed to His servants (Matt. 18:19). He does not mock His people by a call to any work for which He does not fully provide. "God's work done in God's way never lacks God's supply," testified Hudson Taylor; and many other missionaries have proved this to be true.

The idea of planning a career will be radically altered if one recognizes the bondslave relationship to Christ as Master. My worldly reputation will then be dependent entirely upon His purpose for me, as related to publicity and successful achievement. I shall be encouraged, not by statistical superiority of my reports, but by His "Well done!"

In some situations, where the missionary can be a little king in his domain, an original unselfish devotion to the ministry of the gospel becomes modified by the security of a fixed income, by the power of recognized authority over station or church, by the elimination of hard work as servants are at hand. It is possible for a missionary to backslide, and he can become lazy. My motivation is thus not a rigid attitude, incapable of alteration. As long as I live, my eyes must be turned toward Jesus; and the things of this world do grow strangely dim in the light of His glory and grace. Godly motivation is the fruit of a life abiding in Christ. Divine love working through me ensures the fulfillment of divine purpose.

GOAL

THE GRAND STRATEGY of missions derives from the command of the Lord Jesus Christ, "Go ye into all the world, and preach the gospel to every creature" (Mark 16:15).

The life of every Christian should in some way contribute every day to the fulfillment of this command, which has become known as the Great Commission of the church. As military operations are guided by strategic objectives, so the activities of every Christian and of every church need to be evaluated by their contribution to the strategic objective of world evangelization.

The goal of missions will be reached with the end of the age of missions. In sending out His disciples as His witnesses "unto the uttermost part of the earth" (Acts 1:8), Christ went with them (and goes with us) in the person of the Holy Spirit. This age has a promised end, as He indicated: "I am with you alway, even unto the end" (Matt. 28:20). The work of missions is not an unending treadmill. Not only the foretelling and command of the Lord but also the backward look from the end of the age sees "every kindred, and tongue, and people, and nation" represented in the multitude redeemed by the blood of the Lamb (Rev. 5:9).

Such a goal has been variously expressed as the evangelization of the world, or the gathering of the Church out from among all nations, or the completion of the Body of Christ. The great program associated with the return of Christ to earth in person will be the commencement exercises of this period of history. "Then shall the end come" (Matt. 24:14).

There is an ultimate goal beyond the scope of this age. The ultimate is not the concern of missions. It is Christ in person who will have accomplished all that needs to be completed before the end, "when he shall have delivered up the kingdom to God, even the Father" (I Cor. 15:24). The present age of missions is an integral part of God's plan for all history, through which He is answering the prayer taught by Christ, "Thy kingdom come. Thy will be done in earth, as it is in heaven" (Matt. 6:10). The kingdom of God is now imperfectly seen in our midst, and even the end of this age will fall short of the realization of this great goal. It is important to recognize, therefore, that our present objective does not anticipate the Christianization of the world, nor of any nation. The preaching of the gospel has from the beginning called out a divided response: some have mocked in disbelief, some are indifferent, some believe and thus have the right to become the sons of God (John 1:12). The New Testament gives no indication of a general turning to God, but rather the church is pictured as a small company, a group that endures persecution, not holding earthly power. A broad view of the history of the church is hopelessly frustrating when one looks for its increase to ecumenical proportions. It does not even keep pace with increase of population. The goal of world evangelization, however, is increasingly near, and technical developments of the present generation appear as God's provision of a greatly accelerated schedule for the last days, far beyond anything in history.

I. *The Evangelistic Objective*

"Make disciples" is the central command of the Great Commission (Matt. 28:19). Evangelism, or the proclamation of the gospel to the unconverted, is the beginning of making disciples.

The missionary's objective of bringing lost souls to the Saviour may be attained in his own direct encounter with heathenism, or it may be reached indirectly through the ministry of other Christians, who have themselves been taught by the missionary. Both direct and indirect methods will be operating after the first soul is won. Herein is the germ of an indigenous church. Every disciple has the responsibility of witnessing. Self-propagation is not simply a shibboleth of indigenous church policy; it is the very nature of Christianity, and the Christian who is not a witness to Christ before others needs to examine himself regarding his own salvation. It is probable that congregations on the mission fields average a higher concern for witnessing than do the churches of America and Europe. In one country (Korea) it was required that a convert demonstrate genuine faith by bringing at least one other person to Christ before he might be baptized. The missionary who continues to do all the evangelizing, so that new Christians depend on him, is failing in his commission to make disciples.

Development of new means of mass communication has added a new dimension in evangelism. Through literature, radio, recordings and films the living witness has by no means been replaced, but his work has been extended far beyond his bodily presence. These technical specialties, along with transport facilities, have greatly complicated the calls for missionary recruits, and there is a degree of confusion among Christians regarding the call for specialists and also the continuing call for preachers of the gospel. Some emphasize one, some the other. There need be no controversy, since both are required. Every technically trained missionary will share in some measure in evangelism as a personal responsibility, and every evangelist will be aided by technically trained missionaries, at least to the extent of using literature. Certainly there is no point in sending a missionary unless he is able to do work not being done by a national Christian.

II. *The Educational Objective*

Instruction of Christians is also a part of making disciples: "teaching them to observe all things whatsoever I have commanded you" (Matt. 28:20).

1. Biblical Instruction of New Believers. The missionary goal extends beyond the period of spiritual infancy, when a person has entered into the experience of salvation from sin but is not yet able to stand as a soldier of Jesus Christ in the battle against Satan. He must be prepared to receive the strong meat as well as the milk of the Word (Heb. 5:12-14).

God has provided a body of Scripture "profitable for doctrine, for reproof, for correction, for instruction in righteous-ess" (II Tim. 3:16). In the example of the great missionary Paul, we see his concern that young Christians be strengthened as he met them daily for two years (Acts 20:28). His letters to Timothy and to Titus emphasize their responsibility as teachers (I Tim. 4:13; II Tim. 4:2b; Titus 2:1-10).

To teach them to read, and to give them the Bible in their own language must have high priority in the missionary's responsibility to his people. Anything less than strong Christian leaders, able to teach others, is unacceptable as a goal for the missionary church (Heb. 5:12; 6:1).

2. Church Leadership. Special attention needs to be given to the spiritual growth of those whom God raises up as leaders of each local church. Paul's word to Timothy is sharply pointed in directing that what he has learned he must in turn commit "to faithful men, who shall be able to teach others also" (II Tim. 2:2).

The missionary epistles to Timothy and to Titus, describing the qualifications of the bishops or elders or pastors of each church, stated that they must be gifted as teachers (I Tim. 3:2; Titus 1:9). Much of the distress associated with precipitate departure of missionaries at a time of political crisis might be avoided if this scriptural principle of leadership for each congregation were observed from the very beginning. God has provided human leadership in the church with a shepherding and teaching function. The earliest follow-up of the apostles involved the appointment of elders (Acts 14:23). Rather often missionaries have found that the first converts in a new community prove to become such leaders. A chief of police, or mayor, or tribal chief is not uncommonly one of the first believers in a village. Worldly standards of greatness, however, are not acceptable; and the humblest believer may prove to be the one who learns to prevail in prayer and stands true against opposition and becomes the spiritual teacher of the flock. To have discernment in discovering God-given leaders becomes a responsibility of the entire congregation as well as of the missionary. Hunger and thirst after righteousness, faithfulness in study of the Bible, and concern for the salvation of sinners will soon be manifested in such lives. Above all, they will be able to get the guidance of God, and thus make possible a self-governing church, one which is not dependent upon the missionary for knowing the will of God.

A missionary is not excluded from ministry although he is not an officer of the local church. The Church of the Lord Jesus Christ is one. It is not a Japanese, Indian, or American church, depending on geography. Its citizenship is heavenly and its brotherhood includes every child of God. Within the ranks of redeemed souls there is no place for national or racial or social divisions. This makes the Church different from the world, where loyalty to national government and cultural ideals has a useful function. It is transnational or supranational, as well as international.

In their zeal for indigenity, some missionaries have gone to the extreme of separating themselves from the churches among which they are serving. If having the missionaries on the platform and the nationals on the floor has been divisive and paternalistic, what shall we say when missionaries segregate themselves from church meetings entirely? The Body of Christ must not be dismembered; foreign and national Christians together must pray, study, and minister unto the Lord. God will speak to His people through His messengers of all nationalities. "Neither Jew nor Greek, . . . ye are all one in Christ Jesus" (Gal. 3:28).

3. General Education. The education of children is primarily the responsibility of parents (Deut. 6:7). Christian parents in particular must face this responsibility, and the church as a whole will also have a common concern for bringing up its children "in the nurture and admonition of the Lord" (Eph. 6:4).

In the explosive development of nations of this generation, the normal process of teaching by their elders has been lost, and children are growing in a pattern of knowledge and custom which breaks beyond the confines of parental culture. Missions and government have stepped in to provide schools for this orphan generation, apparently justified in such a program, yet not escaping the danger of social dislocation which has been fertile soil for subversive movements beyond all others recorded in history. The "perilous times" have come (II Tim. 3:1).

Missionaries must help their national Christian brethren in every way possible, to provide for general education on a Christian foundation. This is no substitute for Christian family life. To evangelize and educate children without evangelizing their homes is to shelter lambs with wolf-mothers. A child needs its father and mother, and a Christian school is a poor substitute for Christian parents. Home, church and school should together train the child to know God and to serve the Lord Jesus Christ. Only when Christians control the elementary school can they guard the foundations of Christian life among their young people.

Even more in dealing with secondary and higher and technical education, there has not been a clear recognition of Christian responsibility. The trend to government responsibility for education appears to be part of the preparation of the world for atheistic and anti-Christian social controls. The scriptural proverb is clear, that prohibits study under ungodly teachers: "Cease, my son, to hear the instruction that causeth to err from the words of knowledge" (Prov. 19:27). The missionary and the local church will need to get specific guidance as to their duty in general education, and they may be thankful for every school that is available for teaching a Christian culture to their growing generation.

To summarize, it is the responsibility of every Christian home and of every congregation to see that its children get education on a Biblical basis, with Christian teachers and a Christian philosophy of education. The teaching of every subject should be integrated with Biblical truth, for no department of learning is complete without a recognition of

God in it. The missionary will be teaching the church what God expects of them, but his work will be more directly in the training of teachers.

III. *The Ecclesiastical Objective*

The goal of preaching the gospel to all nations involves a separation from the world and unto Christ of all those who respond to the gospel. The description of God's work in the beginning of missions is that He "did visit the Gentiles, to take out of them a people for his name" (Acts 15:14). The Church is clearly a called-out company, belonging to Heaven rather than to earth.

The Church is represented visibly in each community by the group of believers who gather together. A lonely Christian is not a normal Christian. The idea of withdrawal into a monastic life of solitude is not taught in the Bible. Even our Lord went apart only for a limited time, particularly for communion with His Father in prayer, and once, led by the Holy Spirit, he had a personal encounter with the devil.

It is extremely important to recognize the personal activity of Christ in His statement, "I will build my church" (Matt. 16:18). By holding strictly to the principle that the work of missions is the work of Christ, we avoid many pitfalls of missionary activity. Christ is the one doing the work, by the Holy Spirit, and He graciously chooses to use a man, a missionary, as His instrument. The work is not dependent on the man, and the Lord may choose to set him aside. God's work will get done, even if the man fails or moves elsewhere. The omnipotence of God is not frustrated by the small capacity of His messenger. Wherever faith operates, God works.

Since it is Christ who is the architect and builder, missionaries do well to avoid personal and traditional preferences in their counseling with believers. Many accessory activities tend to cling to a given pattern of church life, so that when American missionaries attempt to transplant these forms, a little America appears in the new environment, including all the organizations that Americans so love. The simplicity of the New Testament church stands in sharp contrast to much that has accumulated in the American tradition. It is frequently a painful procedure to separate Biblical from traditional Christianity. The dangers inherent in transplanting American ways are so great, however, that one must be ruthless in insisting on the growth of an indigenous church.

What is an indigenous church? Its classical description as self-supporting, self-governing, and self-propagating expresses the general objective of all sincere missionaries, desiring as they do to see believers become mature in the faith and exercise gifts in the church. The word means simply belonging to a given country. The details of the picture of an indigenous church, however, convey such a variety of interpretations, that little meaning attaches to the word as a statement of policy. It has meant everything from absolute separation of foreign funds from any national work or worker, to the full support of national pastors in their churches through a mission.

The emphasis upon self gives a wrong idea in this definition. In truth, every church needs to recognize its dependence upon God. The church that is able to carry on in self-reliance has ceased from its supernatural character. The description of self-support, self-government, and self-propagation is correct as far as its relation with the mission is concerned; but it is deceptive and fatal when not properly interpreted. A positive statement of dependence upon the Holy Spirit and subjection to the Lord Jesus Christ will express more clearly the missionary ideal.

Self-support should mean a recognition of Biblical standards of stewardship, devotion to the will of God in handling our possessions. When God is in control of the daily life of His people, He always provides the necessary support (Phil.

4:19). A company of tithers never needs to look to the mission or to any other outside source for funds to do God's work.

Self-government should mean the headship of Christ in His Church. As He builds His Church, He likewise gives spiritual gifts, including wisdom and administration (I Cor. 12:8, 28). In the selection of elders in a congregation, these gifts will be recognized, among others, in being shown by experience ("not a novice," "first proved"), and demonstrated ability ("ruleth well his own house") (I Tim. 3:4, 6, 10).

Self-propagation should mean an active witness to Christ by all His people, as well as the gift of an evangelist in some. This is ideally true from the beginning. Certainly there is gross failure when it is indefinitely delayed. Even without public preaching, the godly behavior and the loving attitude of a Christian community are the best of all evangelistic sermons.

Simply stated, an indigenous church is a congregation in which the Holy Spirit has liberty to work, and is not dependent on the presence of missionaries. It lives by a supernatural life. It expects the gifts of God to be manifested within itself. Thus the ideal does not turn on geography or nationality or race. The ideal depends on the control of the Head of the church over each of its members.

When missionaries are taken from a field, God has not failed. They have served as does a scaffolding, which is never intended to support the structure itself and is torn down as soon as possible. Then comes the answer to the question, Upon what foundation have we built, and of what materials? (I Cor. 3:10-15).

IV. *The Philanthropic Objective*

The relief of suffering must be recognized as a fourth objective of missions. It is a part of the "all things" commanded

(Matt. 28:20), and is evidence of the life of Christ in a believer.

Our Lord demonstrated this in His personal ministry, for He was touched by the misery of people, and had compassion on the sick and the suffering. The missionary, as indeed any Christian, provides a channel through which God may be pleased to encourage those in distress, to relieve fears, to meet the needs of suffering minds and bodies. The hungry will be fed, the naked clothed, the homeless sheltered. This ministry is not simply a wedge for the entrance of the gospel; it is an outreach of divine love.

Unfortunate perversions of social service as a substitute for the preaching of repentance and the remission of sins must not be allowed to deprive us of this Christlike activity. On the other hand, we dare not send missionaries merely as doctors, technicians, agriculturalists, and the like. The missionary is a man, a whole man, Christ's man, not merely a machine for performing a certain task. Christ goes in the missionary. Christ is the one who does the work. The work of missions is the work of Christ Himself, utilizing the body and mind of His servants as the contact with a needy world.

Hands of love carry a message that prepares hearts for the coming of the Saviour. The Lord Jesus Christ does not need to be advertised as the one who is the sponsor of the program. By the Holy Spirit He is right at hand, ready to enter and cleanse hearts as they are opened to Him in response to His loving approach. China was opened "at the point of a lancet" by the surgery of Doctor Peter Parker. Such services are an integral part of the message of God. Christ came healing the blind, the lame, lepers and the deaf, raising the dead and preaching the gospel. All this was in His ministry. No less can we as missionaries neglect the temporal needs of the heathen.

Perhaps it will help to clarify the issue by recognizing that the great enemy of Christ is continually troubling mankind, causing every kind of pain. The world of demons seems to delight in human suffering. To relieve such suffering is ministry of the Holy Spirit, who uses lives committed t Christ for His Lordship. A life of obedience to God wil therefore, not fail to include service to others, the only wa in which a man can give service to God.

Each missionary profits from having an individual goal fc the day, the month, the year. Each missionary organizatio should get a clear goal from God as its particular objec tive. The above general objectives unite all the companie of God's army in a common concern for the answer t the prayer taught by our Lord, "Pray ye therefore th Lord of the harvest, that he would send forth labourers (Luke 10:2).

CHAPTER II

MISSIONARY RELATIONSHIPS

Milton Baker

Fortunately, the broad topic listed above has been limited to a few specified areas, particularly missionary relationships to the home church and to the national church. Within this scope it has been suggested that we discuss the questions of the missionary's church membership, which church (home or foreign) should have authority over him, and whether the Christian worker going to a foreign country should carry the familiar title "missionary" or the more recent innovation, "fraternal worker."

All of these questions are part of a larger and very familiar subject of discussion in foreign mission circles: "identification." How can we, as foreigners, most effectively reach the hearts of our listeners with the words of eternal life? Christ set the example of identification, for in coming to earth He set aside His glory, took upon Him the form of a servant, was made in the likeness of men and became obedient unto death (Phil. 2:7-8). He who knew no sin was made sin for us "that we might be made the righteousness of God in him" (II Cor. 5:21). He "was in all points tempted like as we are, yet without sin" (Heb. 4:15).

For the missionary, identification is a twofold challenge. One African Christian put it this way as reported by Bishop Lesslie Newbigin:

> There are two conceptions of identification. There is what I call an anthropological conception of identifica-

tion and there is identification in Christ. It is the second in which we are interested.

"Anthropological identification" is most obvious. It involves the details of being in a foreign country, submerging one's own national heritage and background and adapting to the new environment in a way that people will most readily listen to the gospel message without undue attention being drawn to the "foreign speaker." This aspect of identification involves understanding and appreciating the people and their ways, humility and such practical things as mastering the language and adapting to the cultural habits of the people insofar as no spiritual compromise is involved. This form of identification was practiced by Paul, for, said he, "Though I be free from all men, yet have I made myself servant unto all, that I might gain the more. . . . I am made all things to all men that I might by all means save some" (I Cor. 9:19, 22).

A more difficult aspect of identification involves showing forth "the praises of him who hath called you out of darkness into his marvellous light" (I Peter 2:9). The motto of this identification—"He must increase, but I must decrease" (John 3:30). The means of realizing this identification—abiding in Christ and letting the Word of Christ dwell in us richly in all wisdom (John 15:5; Col. 3:16). The message of this identification—"For we preach not ourselves, but Christ Jesus the Lord; and ourselves your servants for Jesus' sake" (II Cor. 4:5). The goal of this identification—to "present every man perfect in Christ Jesus" (Col. 1:28). The missionary relationships listed at the outset of this paper, therefore, must be handled in a way to most fully realize the goal of identification—to present every man perfect in Christ Jesus.

Missions handle the matter of a missionary's relationship to the sending (home) church and the receiving (national or foreign) church in various ways. In his book *Revolution in Missions* Willis LaMott wrote:

In the former church of Christ in Japan, the four co-operating missions maintained four quite different relationships to the church. In a very few cases, the mission was absorbed into the national church. In some cases clerical missionaries became equal members of the local association or synod; in others they were corresponding members; elsewhere they possessed no ecclesiastical status whatever. In some instances missionaries worked for the church but outside it; in others, with it; in others, under it. However, the situation was saved by the growing conviction that with fellowship all things were possible.

This is a good word. It clearly reveals that the heart relationship is the important thing. If the hearts of the missionaries and the national Christians are bound together by the love of Christ, any arrangement will be satisfactory. However, in many places the desired degree of love between national Christians and missionaries has not yet been realized. It is necessary, therefore, to study which arrangement of mission-church relationships will most rapidly produce the desired goal of "presenting every man perfect in Christ Jesus."

I. *Paul's Relationship to the "Home" Church*

The Book of Acts seems to indicate a definite relationship between the sending church and the sent ones. The Holy Spirit's call for missionary service came not only to Barnabas and Paul but to the church at Antioch (13:2). Further prayer confirmed the call and resulted in the church commending Paul and Barnabas to the Lord for the work to which they had been called (13:3). As they completed their first missionary journey they "sailed to Antioch, from whence they had been recommended to the grace of God for the work which they fulfilled. And when they were come, and had gathered the church together, they rehearsed all that God had done with them . . ." (14:26-27).

As Paul and Silas set forth on another term of "missionary service" they were again "recommended by the brethren unto the grace of God" (15:40). As this journey came to a close they returned to their "home church" (18:22) and undoubtedly again reported the Lord's working through their ministry.

While Paul's journeys kept him in the same locality for as long as two years, there is nothing to indicate that he joined the local church. Rather, his function as a missionary and church establisher gave him a spiritual leadership which organizationally was above and outside the local church although he was united spiritually with all the believers and all the churches as his epistles attest. We also observe that apparently the "support" of the Antioch church was predominantly prayer, for in different places the Word indicates that Paul supported himself financially as he journeyed.

II. *The Relationships of Today's Missionary to the "Home" and National Churches*

A. What are some of the reasons advanced as to why a missionary should place his membership in a national church rather than retain it in his home church?

1. In a world divided into ideological camps and many countries manifesting a hypernationalistic spirit, a foreign missionary joining a local national church demonstrates the supranationalistic character of the Church of Christ—that it is above any one particular country. It gives visible and tangible evidence that Christians, whether foreign or national, are one in Christ.

2. Some mission boards and denominational groups have definite teaching that each member of their particular group should belong to a local church, preferably a church in the

area where the individual lives. Consequently, a foreign missionary who spends most of his years in a foreign land should join a local church in that land.

3. Over the years, especially during the more "paternalistic" era of foreign missions, some boards encouraged their missionaries to join local churches in order that the churches might be controlled and more easily made to observe the distinctives of the sending group.

4. Many national churches are interested in having missionaries become members. It is seriously questioned that the majority of national churches advocate this procedure as a boon to "identification" between foreign missionaries and national Christians. Rather, observation would indicate that many national churches, knowing that the foreign missionary usually teaches that the members should tithe their income and contribute it to the local church, have seen the monetary gain accruing to the national church if the "rich missionary" should join the church and practice his teaching.

B. What are the reasons why a missionary should not join a national church?

1. Perhaps the most valid reason involves studying the function of a missionary. In our day the term is used to designate anyone sent out by a sending board whether their actual work on the field is building houses, keeping books or teaching nationals how to grow food. While all of these and other talents may be used by a missionary, his basic function is an apostolic function—proclaiming the gospel message, discipling those who respond to the invitation, and organizing the believers into local churches—churches which will carry on their work under the leadership and guidance of the Holy Spirit long after the missionary has moved to another area to duplicate the process. While a missionary may live in a specific geographical locality, he works out from that center to evangelize many villages and establish many churches.

Quoting again from LaMott's *Revolution in Missions:*

Problems of church organization were present in the minds of some of the earliest pioneers. William Ward, associate of William Carey, writing in his journal on October 19, 1805, stated in the following words the conclusion reached by the Serampore brethren concerning the organization of the Indian church—"An idea has lately been suggested and agreed amongst us, namely, that in planting separate churches, native pastors shall be chosen, and native deacons; and that the missionaries shall preserve their original character, giving themselves to the planting of new churches, and to the superintending of those already planted." Commenting on this plan, Carey himself wrote, "By this means the unity of the missionary character will be preserved, all the missionaries will still form one body, each one moveable as the good of the cause may require; the different native churches will also naturally learn to care and provide for their ministers, for their church expenses, the raising of places of worship, etc., and the whole administration will assume a native aspect; by which means the inhabitants will more readily identify the cause as belonging to their own nation and their prejudices at falling into the hands of the Europeans will entirely vanish."

Commenting on Carey's statement, LaMott states:

The policy was sound, also in emphasizing the fact that the newly organized congregations shall be free from the taint of foreignism. Had these principles been put into effect universally, missionary history would have assumed a different trend and the problems that were to plague mission-church relations at a later date would have been avoided.

Carey's phrase, "the missionaries shall preserve their original character, giving themselves to the planting of new churches, and to the superintending of those already planted" indicates the uniqueness of foreign missionaries. Sent out by home churches, they are to be used by the Holy Spirit to reproduce, in accordance with Christ's command, other believers and other churches. The choice of Carey's word "superintending" was an unfortunate one. It is a word implying administrative control. This is far different from the spiritual counsel given by a foreign missionary and received by a local national church, not because they have to accept what is spoken by the foreign missionary but because they recognize the spiritual wisdom contained in the counsel.

2. Keeping his membership in the homeland emphasizes the temporary character of a missionary's ministry. It encourages the national churches to look to the Lord instead of to the missionary as the ultimate solution to their questions and problems.

In an address entitled "Mission in Motion" Bishop Lesslie Newbigin states:

> From the beginning Paul treated the Gentile churches as adult churches, he ordained the ministry from among their own people, and committed them to the Lord in whom they had believed. The relationship to paternalism on the one hand and of dependence on the other which has been such a problem in the modern missionary movement never developed between the church of Antioch which sent out Paul and Barnabas and Silas in their missions and the younger churches which came into being through their preaching.

> Their life was built from the beginning on the faith that the living Spirit of God is able to bear His own witness, to give His own gifts to those who turn to Him, and to create His own fresh image—the image of Christ—in each new people that turns to Him.

> I have seen what happens when one takes seriously the promise of the Holy Spirit and, therefore, takes it for granted that He is able to create for these new congregations out of their own people, even though they be simple and illiterate, the kind of pastoral leadership that they need and He can use.

I have seen men who are continuing to earn their own living as ordinary laborers and who have never been inside the walls of a theological college, developing the gifts needed for pastoral oversight of the new congregations and evangelistic witness to those beyond.

There is some validity to the affirmation that conditions on many mission fields are unlike those which Paul found in the course of his missionary journeys. Illiteracy, more extreme forms of heathenism (the Jews and Greek proselytes already believed in one supreme God rather than in many deities), language and cultural barriers are greater in some areas of the world now than where Paul ministered. However, there is also truth in the charge that Christian missionaries underestimate the power of the Holy Spirit. This manifests itself in a tendency, unconscious in most instances no doubt, to encourage national Christians to look to the missionary for guidance and instruction long after they should have received a sufficient knowledge of truth to look directly to the Holy Spirit to teach them from the Word regarding solutions to their problems. Perhaps if from the very outset missionaries would clearly define not only the plan of salvation but also the cost of discipleship, what is involved in the Lordship of Christ and the leadership of the Holy Spirit, many national churches would be stronger and more spiritual by abiding in Christ rather than by constantly seeking the assistance of a foreign missionary.

3. Identification should not be a one-way street. Coming from a large, wealthy, heavily industrialized nation with all of the material comforts derived from such a heritage, we tend to forget that these do not necessarily make Americans more intelligent or more understanding than the people of other races and nationalities. In fact, a national Christian, indwelt by the Holy Spirit, may often understand the implications of rapport, and practice identification with others more readily than many non-Christian Americans. One of the bright spots in the somber situation in the Republic of Congo

since its independence in 1960 has been the oneness which truly dedicated Congolese Christians have had with dedicated missionaries and vice versa. The measure of success in identification is almost in direct proportion to the extent that individuals and groups of differing nationalities and races are willing to become identified with each other. In this regard Canon Max Warren, writing the chapter "The Meaning of Identification" in the book *The Theology of the Christian Mission,* wrote these significant words:

> "Identification with" does not mean loss of identity. It means the sympathetic entering into the life of another. Only by a deep mutuality of relationship can "identification with" be purged of a purely romantic and unreal significance. The missionary who leaves America or Britain for India does not go to meet his Indian colleague bearing all the burden of "identification with" on his own shoulders. Partnership involves for the Indian no less real an adventure of meeting, a no less difficult "identification with" the man from the West. The true dignity of relationship demands the recognition of mutuality.
>
> . . . If identity is retained, as it must be if genuinely reciprocal relationships between church and church are to be realized, then both parties to the meeting have *responsibilities back to those whom they represent* [writer's underlining]. The man from the West retains with his identity his identification with those who have sent him, just as the Indian in our illustration has responsibilities born of his own identification with his own people.

4. For a missionary to join a national church makes it easier to dominate the affairs of the church, even where such domination is not particularly sought after. As Carl Henry stated in his article "Whither 'Ecumenical Mission' ":

> Even where missionaries represent a small minority in the councils of the church, their training and experience, together with the fact that they have often been the teachers of these beside whom they sit . . . would give them an undue influence in directing church policies.

In these days of strong national consciousness on the part of newly independent countries formerly controlled from Europe, anything that would even give the appearance of control should be shunned. While it is true that missionaries can dominate a church without joining it, it is much easier for a missionary who does not want to control the national church to keep his influence at a minimum as a nonmember. To be a member involves the responsibilities of membership: namely, participation in discussion of business matters and voting when a question is to be decided. The mere display of a missionary's hand in voting will influence the sizable group, always found in the local church, which bases its decision on the thinking of a strong personality. Not to be a member of a local church makes it much easier for a missionary to disengage himself from the insignificant and nonspiritual aspects of church life without offending anyone, thus keeping him free to give a positive spiritual ministry to all groups within the church.

In his book *An Introduction to the Science of Missions* Bavinck, in commenting on the role of the sending church, states that it is quite natural in his group for the missionary to preside as the moderator of a newly formed church. He then proceeds to list some of the dangers where this is done:

> 1. If a church is independent, whence does the missionary get his authority to preside? . . . The mother church ought in no wise to interfere with the affairs of the younger church through the missionary, and this holds all the more if a great cultural and racial difference exists which inadvertently places a great deal of strain upon any such relationship.

> 2. A second great danger connected with the continued oversight of the missionary is that the young church is artificially kept immature. . . . The very presence of a missionary, and the very faithfulness of his care, no matter how well intended, may result in impeding the growth of a young church.

3. A third danger is directly related to the missionary himself. He is readily inclined to think of himself as indispensable and to regard the young church as immature. If the moment of his departure depends on him, there is an increasingly real danger that he will continue to postpone it. . . . To be left alone is the only way a church can learn responsibility.

The white race inadvertently has a certain feeling of superiority. It is soon inclined to think that without its own help other races cannot make any progress. Especially where this feeling of superiority is enforced by political control, there is a great chance that the white church will assume it has the right to exercise a long period of guardianship over native churches. In such cases, however, it is well to remember that the Scriptures know nothing of the concept of guardianship within the church. Political norms may never be transferred to the church. The church is a structure of an entirely different nature, and it is on safer ground when it calmly allows itself to be guided by the Scripture and by it alone. And when Scripture is followed the independence and autonomy of the young church is respected from the very beginning. It then has the opportunity to practice bearing its own responsibility, until it is called to go its own way entirely, without the advice of the missionary and the mother church.

Even where national Christians have sufficient spiritual maturity not to be unduly influenced by the missionary's vote if he were to be a member of the local church, his very membership is used as a weapon in the hands of nationalistic non-Christians to accuse the missionaries of tampering with national institutions and accuse the national Christians of being duped by a foreigner.

In his paper "Missions and Nationalism" Rev. Arthur Glasser states:

Indigenous principles are the order of the day. The old paternalism, the "handout" approach of the nineteenth

century, must be completely repudiated. Today all peoples want to be themselves, independent of all other nations, especially independent of the West. We should
respect this.

In countries where, until recently, people have been dominated by foreigners, we would do well not to assume
any semblance of control such as would be indicated by
the missionary joining and taking part in the affairs of a
local church.

5. Spiritual fellowship and spiritual identification with the
people are not dependent upon church membership. Evangelists in America are a familiar illustration of this principle.
They go from church to church, sometimes staying as long as
three or four weeks in one church. They are expected to be
the Lord's messenger in bringing teaching and exhortation
from the Word, they fellowship with the people in their
homes, but it is not thought at all strange that they do not
transfer their church membership. While it is true that they
do not stay in one church as long as a missionary may live
in a given locality on the mission field, close study would
possibly reveal that many missionaries would do well to
move their place of residence from time to time. This not
being possible, they should spend greater amounts of time
in many churches rather than a disproportionate amount of
time in any one church. Where a missionary belongs to a
local church there is danger that the church will speak of
him as "our missionary" to the exclusion of the other churches
ministered to by the missionary. As Dr. Raymond Buker has
put it:

> If he belongs to one local church, the other churches are
> prone to develop jealousies, misunderstandings and di-
> vision because of this uneven relationship to the one. The
> missionary is to be a spiritual adviser to all. He will be
> the sponsor of fellowship between the various groups.
> As an outsider, he will be able to lead in the spiritual

phases more effectively than as a member of one particular group.

III. *Authority and Control Over the Missionary*

This is a complex problem. To some degree the missionary is answerable to the sending church or churches, to his mission board, to his fellow missionaries and to the national churches. Variety characterizes the practices of various boards and almost any practical solution of this problem can be successful, provided a right spirit prevails between missionaries and national churches.

As a generalization, wherever projects are being jointly financed by funds coming from foreign and national sources, it is questionable whether absolute authority should rest in either the missionary organization or in the national churches. Where a church is truly indigenous, the local church should be free from outside control. In church-sponsored projects (i.e., benefiting the local churches but partially sponsored and supported by foreign funds) a "sweet reasonableness" should characterize discussions, and decisions should not be made until a mutual area of agreement has been reached by both missionaries and national Christians. Home boards should establish broad lines of policy for their missionaries, but within these boundaries missionaries should be given freedom of action to work with the national churches as the Holy Spirit leads.

In the placement of missionaries there is danger of the missionary staying too long in one place when the national church prefers that he move to another locality. There is equal danger of a national church desiring the missionary to stay in a given locality when it is quite evident to the missionary that the church would be strengthened if he commended it to the leadership of the Holy Spirit and moved to a new location. In other words, in any given situation it is possible for either the missionaries or the national churches to be wrong; therefore, it is necessary for both groups to be responsive to the leadership of the Holy Spirit rather than either group having authority over the other.

"Missionary" or "Fraternal Worker"

Over the years, the term "missionary" has lost much of its meaning. Originally it was used to designate "one sent" by the Lord and the local churches to bear the gospel to distant lands. Now, to most national non-Christians and even some Christians, "missionary" has become another symbol of the white man's domination of underdeveloped nations. In an attempt to alleviate the current distorted interpretation of the word "missionary," some boards have felt that the designation "fraternal worker" would not only recognize the existence of the national church in so-called heathen lands but would convey the oneness of spirit that should prevail between the Christian coming from a foreign country and the national Christians. Unfortunately, in the estimation of many evangelicals, the gains are not worth the losses. We do not cling to the word "missionary" simply because it is traditional. Rather, it symbolizes and conveys a meaning and concept that cannot be captured by any other word. A missionary is not only one sent forth from one nation to another; he is sent particularly as the "bearer of light and the Light" to the spiritually dark places of the world. This is not meant to imply that the particular country in which he labors has no spiritual light. It means, rather, that those churches which have sent him forth intend that his primary duty should carry him to unevangelized areas rather than to labor among already existing churches. The term "fraternal worker" implies working among people who have already become Christians. That many workers from sending countries are spending too much time working with national Christians rather than evangelizing the unreached multitudes is a major concern of Dr. Donald McGavran. His book *How Churches Grow* contains a chapter entitled "The Tremendous Pressure to 'Perfect.'" In it Dr. McGavran states:

> There is a constitutional bias toward perfecting. The churches gravitate toward caring for what they have. Their built-in nature prefers perfecting. It is easier for the church to settle down to a quiet shepherding of the flock than to climb uphill to missionary endeavor. . . . The pressure to perfect induces the older churches in the West and the East to lavish care on themselves, pressing forward feverishly to better and ever better church buildings, programs, Christian education and service enterprises. It bears down on the vast missionary programme thrusting it ever more certainly into channels of service to the already established younger churches.

Servicing already established churches readily lends itself to fraternal workers but this functional concept is quite different from that which motivates young people to apply to mission boards to reach a lost world in their generation.

Substituting "fraternal worker" for "missionary" may indicate a greater theological problem than many realize. There is an increasing tendency on the part of liberal, ecumenical theologians to look with disfavor upon a theology which designates the peoples of the world as either "saved" or "lost." These men prefer, rather, to think of people as "committed" or "uncommitted" but all as being brothers in Christ. As one writer has put it:

> The radical theologian does not believe that anyone is actually "outside." All are "inside," for God "claimed the whole world for Himself in the death of Jesus." However, some of those "inside" are "committed" and some are "uncommitted." The church's task is no longer to go "outside" and bring lost sheep "in."

Those holding this concept, entirely foreign to the teaching of the Bible, would naturally shun any word that might infer that "saved" people were being sent out to preach to "lost" people. In its place must be a word or phrase which indicates that we are already a "world brotherhood" and that we can all learn from one another by sharing "fraternal workers."

In pleading for the retention of the word "missionary," Dr. Carl Henry wrote:

> There are few countries in which Protestant missionaries are at work today where as many as five percent of the people have been won to the Christian faith. Any philosophy of missions which diverts attention from this unfinished task and interprets our continuing role principally in the terms of interchurch aid must be classified as a major retreat in missionary strategy. Established works should be turned over as rapidly as possible to the indigenous church while the missions move on to the "regions beyond." . . . Our mandate to preach the gospel to the unbelieving people of the world comes from Christ, not from any national church body. We were "sent" before we were "invited," and it is inconceivable that the coming into being of a relatively small body of believers in any country should put an end to the initiative of men and women who have been called of God to preach the gospel to every creature. . . .

Dr. Henry concluded this editorial with the ringing words:

> We can say "fraternal worker" instead of "missionary," and "ecumenical mission" instead of "missions" if we like, but let us remember that we are talking about different things. What "ecumenical mission" will accomplish is not yet clear, but let us not forget that it was "missions"— the business of being sent to the unevangelized—that fired the souls of the apostles and turned the world upside down.

The relationship of a missionary to a national church comprises many involved factors. These, in turn, require the most in spiritual discernment if unnecessary problems would be avoided. In considering these relationships, it would seem wise that a missionary should not hold as his philosophy,

"How close can I get to the people?" but rather should constantly be asking himself, "What can I do to bring the people among whom I live and work to a closer, more intimate relationship with Jesus Christ?"

Melvin L. Hodges

I. *The Relationship of the Missionary to the Home (Sending) Church*

THE CLEAREST PRESENTATION of the relationship of the missionary to the sending church is found in Acts 13 and 15. In Acts 13:1 we find the reference to the leaders of the church in Antioch. Verse 2 states: "And as they ministered to the Lord, and fasted, the Holy Ghost said, Separate me Barnabas and Saul for the work whereunto I have called them. And when they had fasted and prayed, and laid their hands on them, they sent them away. So they, being sent forth by the Holy Ghost, departed. . . ."

The missionary candidates were first of all called by God and sent by the Holy Ghost. Proper emphasis on this important truth will keep missions from degenerating into a merely human activity.

The missionaries were also sent forth by the church. We must maintain the proper emphasis on this truth in order to avoid hurtful individualistic missionary effort.

In Acts 15 we see that the sent ones are responsible in a certain sense to those who sent them. In verse 24 the church of Jerusalem writes to the younger churches, disallowing the ministry of certain ones who went out from the church at Jerusalem without being sent: "To whom we gave no such commandment." And then it proceeds to recommend approved workers (v. 25), chosen men (v. 27): "We have sent therefore Judas and Silas. . . ." The conclusion is inescapable that the missionaries are responsible to someone in their own homeland for what they teach and what they do.

II. *The Relationship of the Missionary to the Field (the Younger Churches)*

The question is frequently raised as to whether a missionary, as such, belongs to a bygone age. In this concept it is considered something of an insult for an older church to send a "missionary" as it would seem to place the younger church in an inferior position. Some churches no longer refer to their missionaries by that name, but insist that they be sent forth as "fraternal workers."

Let us take note of the fact that the relationship of a missionary to a work he raises up in a pioneer field must certainly be different from that of a missionary who comes to a church already organized and established. In the first instance, he is like Paul, a planter; in the second, he is like Apollos, a waterer (I Cor. 3:6). There are many instructors in Christ, but not many fathers (I Cor. 4:15). The titles "missionary" and "apostle" have the same basic meaning: one sent out. The missionary has the apostolic ministry of planting churches. As long as there are areas in the world where the Church of Jesus Christ is not planted, we need missionaries. These missionaries do not necessarily come from one certain country. They may be just as truly sent by God when the sending church is itself a young church, newly founded. The missionary who raises up a pioneer church will have a unique relationship of spiritual father to that church. No other person who may come to the church at a later date will be a missionary to that church in the same sense as the founding missionary.

As the young churches develop in self-government, they have a right to make their own decisions. Though Paul was a "father" to many of the New Testament churches, it is to be noted that he refrained from urging the church to action on the basis of a father-and-son relationship. Rather, he pointed the converts to Christ and he besought them and pleaded with them that they would take a certain course of action for Christ's sake. Certainly, there is no New Testament basis for the younger churches being made subordinate to the older churches in the homeland and being controlled by missionaries who are not even the fathers of the work.

While the principal ministry of the missionary is apostolic in the sense of founding churches, there are also watering ministries to the young church. Missionaries today are sent out to help a church that is already founded by providing instruction for young ministers, technical knowledge in literature distribution, and giving counsel to native pastors and young churches. In this sense the Apolloses, Timothys and Tituses of the Book of Acts were also missionaries. However, these men were recruited from among the young churches, rather than from Jerusalem or Antioch. These missionaries, whose primary ministry is not that of founding churches but of encouraging the growth of churches already established, could well be described by the term "fraternal workers." This is a correct term insofar as it reveals that the purpose of the missionary is not to rule or govern the young church, but to assist in its growth. In such a category, the missionary is a guest of the church that he is serving. The term "fraternal worker" is, however, inadequate if it is applied to the missionary effort that is primarily the raising up of churches in an area that has not been evangelized.

In some quarters there is still objection to the thought of turning over authority to the young church, and it is felt that the work is only safe as long as a missionary is at the helm. To such I would point out that control imposed on the church by the missionary is, in the long run, of little value. The missionary can control properties and funds that pass through his hands. He cannot, however, really control the church. The church must in its own right grow up to the measure of the stature of the fullness of Christ and carry on as an adequate part of the Body of Christ. Many a missionary has made the fatal mistake of commanding when he should have pled with his converts "for Christ's sake." Our only real hold on the work, as missionaries, is what we enjoy because of our spiritual life, influence, and ministry. If we cannot in the Holy Spirit appeal to the church to do something for Christ's sake and be obeyed, then authority that is based on the control of property or on the handling of finance is of little real permanent spiritual value.

Most missionaries realize that they are not necessarily accepted, nor should they expect to be accepted by the national church, simply on the basis of the fact that they are foreigners or missionaries. Every missionary must win for himself his proper place in the church by virtue of his life and ministry. Spiritual ties and spiritual influence are stronger than any other, and in the long run are the only ones that count.

The question has often been asked, What should the relationship of the missionary be to the church which he founds? Should he become a member of the local church which he has raised up? No categorical answer could hope to win the approval of all as our opinions on this matter will be largely the result of our varied concepts of church government. My own personal viewpoint is that the missionary should identify himself completely with the national church as far as responsibilities, oneness of purpose, spiritual ministry, and financial contributions are concerned. However, I question the wisdom of a missionary taking too active a part in a local church. If he becomes a member of the local church, it should be for the spiritual benefits he can receive and give, but it would be well for him to refrain from exercising full rights of membership in matters of voting, administration, holding local church offices, and so forth. Furthermore, it may be quite difficult for him to fulfill the financial obligation required of ordinary members. His finances may very well belong to the work as a whole, rather than to one local church. For a missionary to become a full-fledged member of a local church would automatically require that he fill offices in the church and give regular financial support as would be required of any other member. I do not feel that this is a correct relationship. Because of his superior ability and experience, because of his financial contributions, the missionary would logically soon be filling a place in the church far out of proportion to that which a regular member would fill. In fact, he might soon be actually administering the affairs of the church from behind the scenes, even though the church had its own national pastor and counseling committee.

In our own work we have made it a practice to encourage the missionaries to take their place in the national church on the same level as a national minister. In our particular organizational plan, we give room for the sovereignty of the local church, but at the same time bind these churches together in a national organization, in which both churches and ministers hold membership. We feel that this is the proper place for the missionary to have membership. In this position he can support the work as a whole with his finances and add the strength of his spiritual ministry and experience without unduly influencing the administration of the local churches or the work in general. On the convention floor he will be able to speak his convictions. In the voting he will have one vote the same as any other minister. If he is chosen to fill an executive office in the national organization, it will be because he has gained the confidence of his fellow ministers and not because he is placed in command of the church by a foreign missions board.

An interesting picture of the influence of the missionary, the Apostle Paul, in the local church of Corinth, is seen in I Corinthians 5. Here was a serious problem of discipline in which the membership of an individual Christian was at stake and the testimony of the whole church was in the balance. What did the apostle do? He did not remain entirely aloof from the problem. He gave them instruction and exhorted them to faithfully fulfill their duties. He thrust the responsibility of discipline squarely upon the church itself.

"When you come together to consider this," he said in effect, "just think that I am there in spirit with you, and deal with the matter in the name of the Lord Jesus Christ with the recognition that God's Spirit is among you." He taught them, he exhorted them, he gave them his example but he did not do the task for them. He let them take their proper responsibility and fulfill their own proper function.

This in brief gives a beautiful picture of a father exhorting his spiritual sons but at the same time recognizing that these children have come of age and now must take the responsibility of managing their own affairs.

J. F. Shepherd

Missionary," "missions," and particularly "foreign missions" are terms which have had an honorable place in Christian vocabulary, but lately their use is being called in question. Most of this criticism arises out of zeal for ecumenical organization. While it is not a flat rejection of all organized efforts for world evangelization, it does insist that the traditional patterns for such work are improper. Objections are raised to the conception of the "missionary" as one whose function and relationships distinguish him from the regular ministry of the national church which he serves on the field. Moreover, it is contended there is no justification for the maintenance of "missions" as organizations existing alongside the national church.

I. *What About the Term "Foreign Missions"?*

The strongest antagonism is against the use of the term "foreign missions." Many of the protagonists of ecumenism seem convinced that it is impossible to speak of foreign missions without conscious discrimination. In support of the ecumenical viewpoint, elaborate arguments about the nature of the church and the nature of the ministry are brought forward against traditional missions terminology and organization. It may be that real motivation is more for monopoly in ecclesiastical administration than for theological purity and Biblical consistency.

Evangelicals of nonecumenical persuasion can hardly make a case for their present administrative patterns in the conduct of missions as being in explicit conformity to any New Testament practice or doctrine, but it does seem certain that the methods they advocate can be shown to be consistent with Biblical principles. Missions as sending agencies or missionaries as persons whom they recruited, hired, and sent do not appear on the pages of the Bible. Neither is there absolute Biblical basis to distinguish "home" and "foreign" in the mission of the church. Nonetheless, the organizations and methods characteristic of the modern missionary enterprise will stand up under Biblical appraisal as a legitimate means for the accomplishment of what the Bible teaches to be the will of God in proclaiming the gospel in all the world.

Since Carey's time, and even before, Protestant churches in the West have sought to reach people in Asia and Africa and other parts of the world with the gospel. This work was carried out, for the most part, through cooperative societies or boards, some of which were organically related to denominations or established churches and some of which were independent. Quite naturally these groups came to be called "missions," and the work of missions in foreign parts was almost completely identified with their activities.

The term "missions" came inevitably to refer to this specialized activity of the church rather than to the general responsibility of Christians to witness for Christ. In this sense the usage was functional rather than theological; missions was one of the methods of the church's witness relative to the historical and geographical situation. In relating this particular type of ministry to the totality of the work of the church, the purpose of missions came to be regarded as more comprehensive than simply bearing witness for Christ and saving souls. In the course of these developments, the term "missions" came to be applied to the organized efforts of the church to send the gospel out to those who were uninformed of and unconcerned with the message of the Saviour for the purpose of establishing a church made up of those who received and obeyed Christ as Lord.

Since this outreach of missions was to other lands and cultures distinct from those of the sending group, the adjective "foreign" was fittingly descriptive and in no sense derogatory. Actually this was in agreement with Scripture, in that the people of God, according to Old Testament and New, were clearly responsible to take the knowledge of God to other nations and peoples. Foreign missions was never fixed or qualitative, but was the dynamic continuity established when those who were reached with the gospel reached on out to others foreign to them. It was natural and unavoidable that the spiritual impulses and spontaneous processes of missions should have come to be institutionalized as mission boards and societies. These organizations soon came to occupy a rather ambiguous position in the life of the church. They were not by nature a church, and yet they served the church in one of its most important functions, and in that very service they became the means for the planting and growth of new churches.

II. *The Missionary as the Middleman*

In this type of situation, the missionary was the man in the middle. He was involved in both the home church and the field church and yet he did not fully belong to either. In a very practical way the relationships of the missionary came to be expressive of the ecclesiastical and administrative align-nent of the church on the foreign field and the sending church through which it came into being.

The ecumenical solution to this increasingly complex situation is that missions, as such, should cease to exist, especially since the church may be said to have been planted in almost all the world. Missions, according to such proposals, with their affairs and personnel should be integrated completely into the churches on the field. Space can hardly be devoted here to an adequate discussion of the ways in which this kind of integration is a threat to all those areas of the life of a national church in which there should be progress toward being indigenous. While the New Testament churches were clearly related in fellowship and interdependence there is an evident restraint on the part of the apostles that seemed to keep them from direct participation in the affairs of the young churches. The modern mission and missionary should conform to that New Testament example, being alongside to help and yet not ruling over or restricted to or dependent upon the so-called younger churches. This is best done by having mission and church as separate and distinct organizations.

If this latter view of mission-church relations is the proper one, it points the way toward some standards for the missionary's relationships. These will vary a great deal according to the national situation, the age and strength of the church, and other factors. While the ultimate objective should be the elimination of the foreign mission, as long as its ministry is needed and desired by the church, the missionary should continue to bear a distinct relationship to both.

Perhaps one important element in a definition of a missionary would be that his financial support is provided by one group to enable him to minister to another. This kind of arrangement is in contrast to the New Testament standard of the church providing for the elder who ministers directly to it. Because of this Scriptural principle the missionary seeks to establish churches that will maintain their own pastors and teachers. This financial aspect of missionary relationship points up the fact that his is a kind of interim function to be terminated when a permanent and proper pattern of church-supported ministry has been initiated. The impracticality of mission-church integration for the conduct of such business seems evident.

The fact that the sending group is the source of the missionary's support places him under a certain responsibility to them and at the same time gives them a sense of sharing in his work and fulfilling their missionary obligation through him. His contact with the home church is carefully maintained so as to insure prayer support and to work out practical arrangements for furlough, deputation ministry, and the like. The exact nature of the home constituency may range from the home church congregation of which the missionary is a member to a denomination which sends workers with the collective support of associated churches. It may also be that one local church or several congregations will cooperate in sending the missionary through a "faith" board. In any case the missionary stands in a very important relationship to the human agency through which the Lord sends him to the field.

To speak of the relationship of the missionary to the church on the field raises the question as to whether reference is to a local congregation or to some national church organization. Usually it is to some type of national organization that the missionary as a missionary is related. The dangerous tendency to encourage the development of expensive Western-type organizations for church administration is accelerated when mission matters are merged into national church affairs. Is it not better that the church should be kept free from the detailed involvements of location and maintenance of a foreign community? Let the mission manage its own business, making available to the church all of its resources for service in the person of its missionaries without the economic and administrative complications they represent.

There is a wide variety of opinion on this point, but it seems essential today that the national church have a voice in the acceptance of every missionary as well as his field allocation. However, the very principles which argue for continuity of missions with the church would disallow missionary allocation by the church in unilateral action as being the best policy. The vision and program of the mission for an entire country or broad area should not be limited to the outlook and capability of a young church for ministry and evangelism. While the mission shares fraternally in all phases of the ministry of the church in a certain locality, it may well be that as a mission it should be reaching on out to regions beyond without taxing the young church with involvement in the new venture. All of this must be worked out with care and consideration remembering (and it is to the credit of the ecumenically-minded that they constantly emphasize it) that missionaries are guests in the country where they are and that they are there to serve the church, not to manage it.

Many missionaries today who labor in an area where the church is well developed and relatively self-sufficient may experience periods of frustration in which they wonder what they are around for. The regular pastoral positions in the churches are filled by nationals and many other ministries are being taken up by those with competence and training. The efficient missionary must come with spiritual gifts and thorough training with which he can enrich and benefit the church. Moreover these qualities need to be manifest in such a way that those responsible in the church will recognize them and solicit their use and service.

On the level of local church fellowship, if membership is stressed, it would seem that the missionary should take up responsibilties in membership along with fellow Christians.

It is logical and legal that authority and control of the

missionary should rest with those who provide his support and to whom he pledges his loyalty in entering missionary service. However, those missions that are alert to the proper character of growing churches are quick to urge their missionaries to submit to the field church in all matters consistent with Scripture within the proper limits of church jurisdiction.

The attempts to overhaul missionary nomenclature have been rather equivocal. If ecumenical spokesmen would discard the traditional terms once for all, they could be loyally retained by those who still regard them as sound and significant. This would greatly clarify the situation. There would be those on the one hand whose purpose is "ecumenical" with appropriate terminology and those who were "missionary" in the historic sense. Unfortunately, and yet with evidence of admirable honesty, the most effective spokesmen in the missionary areas of the ecumenical movement are really reluctant to relinquish the terms "missions" and "missionary." Even they find "interchurch aid" and "fraternal workers" are inadequate—not to say insipid—substitutes.

Whether or not "missionary" would be a correct rendering for the New Testament "apostle," the word has a distinctly Biblical flavor. That which characterizes the missionary best is that he is a "sent one." He epitomizes the urgency of the sending mission of the church in the world. To those by whom he is sent he is the symbol of outreach to those who need Christ and do not know Him. To those to whom he is sent he is the evidence of loving Christian concern. Perhaps the constant "going" of the missionary is demonstrated in his not quite belonging to either the group who sends or those to whom he is sent and yet he belongs properly and profoundly to both. "Fraternal worker" is a fine phrase and it fits the missionary, but he is more than a brother who shares in the labor of the church on the field. His presence insistently announces that others like himself should leave the ranks of the brotherhood and be sent out to those who are not as yet within the "household of God."

Admittedly there are many aspects of the missionary program that have been all too human and even sinful. There has been the whole tragic list of charges of missionary imperialism, colonialism and paternalism which deserved the severe censure they have received. All of this will not be rectified by revision of terminology. "Missions" and "missionary" are noble words and their use and the tasks they describe should be retained and multiplied by the church. The modern missionary may find life and service in the area between church and mission difficult but it may prove to be a place of "creative tension." Perhaps continuing service here will open up an unexplored dimension of the missionary relationship Jesus described when He said, "As my Father hath sent me, even so send I you."

Timothy M. Warner

IN TURNING TO THE SCRIPTURES for guidance in relation to missions, one must keep in mind that the Scriptures give us principles to be followed rather than an exact pattern to be copied. This is one of the superior qualities of Christianity. Most of the other so-called great religions run into difficulty on this score. Islam, for example, purports to give exact patterns to be followed in almost every area of life, but many things which were compatible with seventh-century Arabian culture do not fit contemporary cultures. As a result, some of these precise formulae for life are having to be changed, and some of the leaders in the Islamic world are currently seeking to reinterpret the teachings of their prophet in order to bring them more into line with contemporary cultural developments. The slavish following of prescribed social conduct has tended to retard progress and to lessen the appeal of this religion to some segments of the modern world.

Christianity, on the other hand, did not set rigid patterns of conduct in the various areas of life. On the contrary, Christ gave great principles to be followed under the dynamic leadership of the Holy Spirit. He gave, for example, virtually no indication as to what form of church government should be instituted by His followers. He commanded His disciples to go into all the world and make disciples of all nations, but He did not spell out how this should be done. What we observe in the New Testament by way of missionary activity is the application to that age of the principles which the early church understood to have been taught by Christ. Just as we see God speaking to His people in the Old Testament through Semitic forms of social and political organization, so we see the church in the New Testament following God's guidance in forms that were culturally relevant to that age. It is with this in mind that we approach the subject of missionary relationships.

I. *Cross-Cultural Relationships*

"It is fundamental to remember that the only persons in this world who are absolutely independent are savages and hermits. The rest of us are set in relations to our fellow men." So states Arthur Brown in his timeless work, *The Foreign Missionary* (p. 237), and some might choose to argue about the validity of the two exceptions he cites. Nevertheless, the fact is basic that we are social beings. The two great commandments of Scripture (Matt. 22:36-39) presuppose man as a social creature with relations to both his Creator and to his fellow creatures. If this is true of all men, it is also true of missionaries.

By placing a man in the role of a missionary, however, certain of the more normal human relationships are greatly complicated; and by bringing two divergent cultures into contact, a whole new set of relationships is introduced.

It has been pointed out (see Per Hassing, " 'At Home' and 'Abroad' in the Missionary's Life," *International Review of Missions*, April, 1955, pp. 182-184) that basic to much of the tension and resulting fatigue of the missionary may be the abnormal relationships which he sustains to the two cultures between which he is forced to divide and to share his loyalties. On the field he attempts to identify himself with those to whom he ministers, but in very rare instances does he actually become a citizen of his adopted country and participate fully in its life. At the same time he is unable to discharge many of the responsibilities of citizenship in his homeland. When he sits down to read, the material is more often than not from "home," although he has been living all day in an entirely different culture. On the other hand, when he returns to his own country, as our system of furloughs necessitates, he is marked as someone a bit different and is constantly being faced with the query, "When are you going back?" He is thus unable to maintain a normal relationship with either culture.

This may be seen reflected in the life of the great missionary apostle. Paul seriously attempted to identify himself with those to whom he ministered, to become "all things to all men," but in so doing he ran into difficulties. By identifying himself with the Gentiles, he incurred the distrust, if not the displeasure, of the Jews. When he returned to Jerusalem and took a Jewish vow, he opened himself to criticism from Gentile sources, in our day if not in his own. Thus a missionary may become a "man without a country" as he tries to maintain ties with two.

This, then, is one of the basic facts to be faced and to which an adjustment must be made by those participating in missionary service; and, in the light of this situation, certain other relationships must be viewed.

II. *Relationship to Sending Church*

Two institutions in two different cultures play a part in the experience of every missionary—the church in the homeland and the church on the field. We are, of course, thinking of the church in a limited way as an organization rather than in a broader sense as an organism. These churches are sometimes referred to as "older" and "younger." This distinction did not exist in the New Testament. At least within the Pauline period they were all first-generation churches. The only significant distinction between them would seem to be that some had a Jewish background and were therefore part of a religious continuum, while the Gentile churches did not have this supposed advantage. When we think of a church that would correspond to the "older" or "sending" church in the New Testament, we think first of Syrian Antioch, which was primarily a Gentile church. Hence the missionary in that day was not faced with quite the same situation as exists today. It was not a case of a person going from a well-established church in an advanced technological economy to a nascent church in a less complex, often subsistence-level economy. Granted that this is not always the case in missionary work today, it is the case more often than not. What should be the relationship of the missionary to each of these churches?

It would appear that the primary relationship between the church in Antioch and the missionaries who went out from it was a spiritual one. They were set apart by the church in response to the leading of the Spirit, and they were sent forth undergirded by the prayers of the church. At the end of their first "term" they returned to report how God had answered those prayers. They had been sent out as stewards of a spiritual message, and they returned to give an account of their stewardship (Acts 13:1-4; 14:26-28).

There seems to be no indication of material support on the part of the church, and the question naturally arises: Is this the pattern to be followed by missionaries today? A slavish imitation of New Testament experience would indicate an affirmative answer. It should be remembered, however, that the culture of Paul's day was very different from that of our own. It was not only customary but almost obligatory for every man to have a trade by which to support himself. While these trades were not always engaged in by men of Paul's educational stature, it was honorable to do so. The societies to which Paul went were all very similar, and he could engage profitably in his trade without being accused of taking money out of the country or of depriving a national of employment. He would not be charged with being a part of a scheme of economic exploitation of the Western nations nor a part of the propaganda machine of a rival power.

Today the picture is quite different. It is not customary for every man to have a trade by which to support himself while doing missionary work as we know it today. Economic factors would make it highly impractical for a person doing some of the specialized ministries of modern missions to attempt to support himself and his family on the side. Thus the missionary looks to the sending church for financial support, and an additional factor is added to his stewardship. A husband, wife, and two children going to the field for four years may represent an investment on the part of the home church of from twenty-five thousand to thirty thousand dollars; and in our economy-minded age, the home church is rightly looking for a return on such an investment—not a financial dividend, but a corresponding investment of life in the souls of men. The missionary, then, cannot think of himself as in any way independent of the home church. The church sends him out and it channels spiritual as well as material resources to him.

In the light of this, the practical implications would seem to be obvious. The missionary must keep the home church informed; he must keep them up to date on his work so that they may pray intelligently. He must attempt to provide the motivation needed by those who routinely carry on the activities necessary to make his more dramatic work possible. The many considerations in the day-to-day outworking of this relationship are carefully discussed in a number of books written for the prospective missionary.

III. *Relationship to Younger Church*

What then is to be the relationship of the missionary to the younger church? In the summary of the work of Barnabas and Paul at the end of their first missionary journey, the verbs used give us a clue to the relationship which they sustained to the churches which they had established. In Acts 14:21-23 we find the following verbs: preached, taught, confirming, exhorting, ordained, prayed, commended. These may be summarized by saying that they sought to help these people establish and develop a vital, dynamic relationship to God through Christ so that He could guide them in the further development of the church. They so taught them that they would be able to translate the principles of the gospel into their own daily experience. They prepared the believers for suffering; they appointed leaders; and then they committed them to God with the confidence that God was faithful and would continue to lead them by His Spirit in the right path.

Paul did not sever all connections with the churches he brought to birth, however. He revisited them and he corresponded with them. When they asked him about a particular problem, he would give them an answer; but he usually did so by using a larger principle which they could then apply to other such situations. Consider I Corinthians, chapters 8-10, where Paul discusses the matter of believers eating meat which had been offered in sacrifice to idols. He answers the basic question clearly, but he leaves them with the principle that "whether . . . ye eat, or drink, or whatsoever ye do, do all to the glory of God. Give none offence, neither to the Jews, nor to the Gentiles, nor to the church of God: . . . that they may be saved" (I Cor. 10:31-33). In establishing this principle he takes them to the Old Testament to show them how it worked out in the experience of the Israelites. When they insisted on their own rights, they could not at the same time bring glory to God nor could they bear the testimony to the nations about them which God had intended. The young church therefore had an answer to its question, but it also had a scriptural principle to apply to similar situations.

It follows, then, that the relationship of the missionary to the young church must be deeply spiritual. He must be certain that the relationship between these people and the Lord is deep and meaningful, that they are not depending on him as an intermediary to interpret God's will for them, that he is not a puppeteer pulling the strings from behind the scenes but afraid to let loose of the strings for fear the puppets will not perform exactly to his liking. He must help them learn to handle God's Word in such a way that they will be able to translate the gospel out of its Jewish setting into their own cultural setting. If done properly, the latter will probably not be as difficult as translating it out of its American setting.

If the missionary has done his evangelizing and his teaching well, he will then be able to trust the Holy Spirit to perfect that which is lacking even though the missionary himself is not present. Paul was willing to let the churches which he brought to birth make some mistakes—even some very serious mistakes. How else could they learn responsibility? A child who is not permitted to go swimming until he learns to swim will never go swimming. He may read books about it and go through the motions on dry land, but not until he commits himself to the water and thrashes around a while will he learn to swim. True, he will need someone with him at first, but his goal should be to become that someone who can teach another. That will never happen if he does not become independent of his teacher. It may well be that the motivation for developing leadership and skill in the ministries of the church has been thwarted by the continual presence of someone who could obviously do it better and faster.

The question is sometimes raised as to whether the missionary should hold his membership in the home church or in the church where he is ministering. We get little guidance from Scripture on this point because the early church probably did not have formalized church membership with church letters and all, but it would certainly seem inadvisable for the missionary to hold membership in the younger church for several reasons. One is that given above, namely, that his presence would tend to thwart the development of indigenous leadership. Another is that if he were to channel all his giving through that church, it would in many instances amount to almost as much as that given by all the other members combined. Even if it were a much smaller percentage, it would tend to throw the church into an economic tailspin if the missionary were to leave. What is perhaps more basic, however, is that unless the missionary were able to identify fully with the culture in which the church was located, his basis for participation in matters such as church discipline would be inadequate. It would be too easy for the local Christians to say, "But you don't understand," and for the person involved to feel that he was being judged by an outsider rather than by his own people. Furthermore, if he were to become a member of the church on the field and continue to receive financial support from the sending church, a number of economic problems would be created.

IV. *Missionary or Fraternal Worker*

What happens when the church becomes truly autonomous and says to the missionary, "We no longer need you as a missionary. We are a part of "the church" and are no longer the object of missionary work. We will rather be participating in the larger mission of the church. If you wish to work with us and in some cases under us, we will be glad for your assistance. If not, we will have to ask you to leave"? In other words, he is no longer a missionary but a fraternal worker. This is a valid development in the life of a growing church. It should be the missionary's aim to bring the church to this point.

The difficulty with the fraternal worker concept as we know it today arises when at a certain historical juncture we are supposed to move across the board from a missionary principle to the fraternal worker principle. A fraternal worker is one who is invited to assist an existing autonomous church. A missionary is one who is sent to bring men and churches to spiritual birth and to see that they are nourished and trained until they reach spiritual adulthood. To say that we can now go only where we are invited is to say that there is no significant area of the world without an established church which has an adequate plan and program for evangelizing the unreached in that area. The New Testament says very little about one church inviting another to send it assistance, but it says a great deal about sending men to reach the lost. Brothers in Christ will naturally help one another. This is one of the basic laws of Christ. It may be that a church will need help with its missionary program, but at some point there will be missionaries who are sent to unreached groups. Until the Great Commission is revoked we must go not just where we are invited, but where there are those who have not heard of a God of love who sent His Son to be their Saviour.

The problem of competition and duplication of effort between missions is often raised, and if there is actually duplication of effort, this should be avoided. Paul certainly sought to avoid this (Rom. 15:20). But there is a vast difference between proclaiming a life-giving message of redemption in the power of the Spirit and presenting a program of "Christian" social action. Ideally the two go together, but it seems that there has been a tendency on the part of some to move toward one of the two poles. If the life-giving message is not being presented, it is not duplication of effort to give it. In the discussion of goals it was pointed out that our aim is to evangelize, not to Christianize. There is no indication in Scripture that the world will be Christianized in this age, but there is a command that it must be evangelized. To try to make society Christian without redeemed men and women as the starting point is futile. With this in mind it is obvious that there are many areas in our world which need "sent ones," men with a life-giving message, because if we wait until we receive an invitation, we may never go.

V. *Relationships Within the Mission*

In this discussion of missionary relationships there remains the significant area of interpersonal relationships—missionary to missionary, missionary to his superior in the mission, veteran to recruit, and so on. Again Brown suggests in *The Foreign Missionary*, page 237, that "the higher we rise in the scale of civilization and of Christian service, the more close and complicated these relations become." These relationships have been discussed at some length by various writers, but experience seems to indicate that we still have much to learn or perhaps to put into practice in this realm.

It must be remembered that missionaries are leaders whether they want to be or not. They have to make decisions whether they want to or not. But at the same time they are men under authority. They must abide by the decisions of the board and the field committee. It is difficult for some to keep these two roles separated, and it may be that in some instances one far outweighs the other. The activity of the missionary may be so regulated that there is no room for personal initiative. (See Paul Clasper, "The Organisation Missionary," *Frontier*, October, 1958, pp. 281-285). On the other hand, the missionary must remember that he applied to work with this particular organization, and its policies are to be fully supported and implemented until they are changed by proper means.

Basic to keeping this relationship between a missionary and those in authority over him in good working order is good communications. The international nature of mission work and the relative isolation in which much mission work is carried on make this a difficult goal to achieve. Decisions made on the basis of incomplete or faulty information do not make for harmony or success, however, and every effort must be expended to insure an adequate flow of facts in both directions. With this in mind, the frequent deputational visits to the fields on the part of responsible persons from the home end are not only justifiable but essential. When the Jerusalem council arrived at its decision, it did so only after hearing personally from those involved in the controversy; and when the decision was to be conveyed to the churches, it could have been done via letter or by the mouth of Paul and Barnabas. But the church decided to send Judas and Silas as well. A vital board decision on a matter of policy can be conveyed to the field in a letter, but the missionaries can not ask a letter questions. A full communication of the meaning and intent of such decisions can probably only be achieved by the method used by the Jerusalem council.

In the matter of human differences or personality problems, as we sometimes call them, there is usually room for improvement on both sides. For one thing, we need a greater degree of spiritual and mental maturity in accepting the fact that such differences do exist in the providence of God and that they evidently exist for a purpose. At the same time, when two supposedly Spirit-filled men cannot get along, it would seem to indicate that the spirit is not the Spirit of Christ who prayed that we might be one (John 17:21).

Relationship to God

All of this leads to the basic relationship, namely, that between the missionary and his Lord. If this relationship is vital and dynamic, God will be able to guide His follower safely and victoriously through a life of ministry on the mission field. God will not lead him into narrowness or stagnation. On the contrary, He will keep the missionary wide-awake to every opportunity to make himself a better vessel for his Master's use. He will keep him intellectually alert and psychologically stable. He will equip him to enter into every other relationship in a constructive and effective manner.

CHAPTER III

INTERNATIONAL COOPERATION

I. *A CONSIDERATION OF PRINCIPLES IN MISSIONS-CHURCH RELATIONS*

Arthur M. Climenhaga and *Edwin E. Jacques*

A MAJOR SEGMENT of concern in the area of interchurch relations today is the question of the relationship between a parent mission organization and the new national church resulting from the decades of missions evangelism. What is the posture of the parent mission to be today with respect to its offspring—the resulting organized church? What shall be the understandings in a broad range of involvements governing mission-church relations? What shall the attitude of the national church be toward the missionaries of the extant mission body?

Several things should be clear at the start in this consideration. First, we shall attempt to deal with broad principles, not specific answers to specific problems. We are not trying to give a final dictum to such detailed questions as who shall or will ultimately own mission property—the mission or the church. While these are issues which have to be faced, the answer to them can only be based on an understanding of broader and deeper implications. (In a sense the same is true of the problem of church membership of the missionary:

Shall it be maintained with a "home" church or should it be transferred to the national church where he is serving?)

Again, the fact of the establishment of an indigenous church is taken for granted. The type of church government is outside the area of our concern. The method and phasing of the national church is only incidental to the central area of concern. The question of the interrelations of the young church with other churches both nationally and supranationally has been discussed in another chapter.

The basic consideration is sharply defined in these terms— a consideration of principles in missions-church relations.

In looking at what has been happening in all mission areas of the world, it seems evident that three patterns of mission-church relationship have emerged. First and historically, there has been missionary superintendence or direction of the life of the newly born church. With few exceptions this apparently was inevitable in the initial stages of the work. However certain mission bodies still continue this method on the grounds that as long as foreign (home-base) funds are used in the program of the mission church, the mission administration will have to control the direction of the church program. National leaders will not be allowed to assume full responsibility until they can achieve comparable education and experience to that of the missionary administration and until they can produce adequate financial resources to operate as an indigenous unit.

Second, there is the opposite development in which the national church leadership demands and in many instances has been given both total church superintendence and missions direction. In many of these cases, such leadership has requested the continuance of foreign subsidies but has taken an ambivalent position in asking missionaries either to go home or to remain but in subservience to the national church program.

Third, we have a development of cooperation between the mission and the church with a pooling of both human and financial resources, insights and consecration, in order to perform jointly the program of church growth and evangelism which neither in today's world could adequately accomplish alone.

As we look at these three patterns, we recognize that modification and shades of variation may exist all along the line. In order to assess the picture in the limited compass of a chapter we are holding our discussion arbitrarily to these three areas with our assessment as to the involvements of each and our conclusion as to principles to be observed.

A. *Missionary Administration in the Church*

The first position of continuing total mission administration over the national church may have even yet a limited number of advocates but in face of the worldwide surging thrust of new nationalisms and political upheavals, the practitioners are decreasing at a quickening pace. We have no modern quotations of note at hand to support or elucidate the continuance of such administrative practice. We thus summarily dismiss the position as having no further pertinence in our consideration.

B. *National Leadership in the Church*

The second pattern—total national church control—is expressed in essence in the following quotation from a speech delivered at a conference in Limuru, Kenya, in 1962. While localized to the African scene, the general philosophy expressed is found in many fields, whether Afro-Asia, South America, or Far East. The speaker said:

> In Africa we find the missions in varying stages of integration with the respective churches. It is still a real issue and must be worked out vigorously and realistically as quickly as possible. Our experiences in India follow very closely the patterns that are developing here in

Africa. They are some of the very same principles, fears, problems expressed here in Africa the past two weeks. For many years there had been a struggle between the mission and church. The mission wanted to bring the church into the mission in one way or another, or wanted complete separation of mission and church. But the church wanted the mission and missionaries to be completely integrated into the church. By 1952, the church won out and the mission integrated into the church.

What is it that the young churches want? Not indigenization in the older sense that we missionaries used to use it. They do not want a self-supporting, self-governing, self-propagating type of church that separates mission and church, missionaries and nationals.

At an African luncheon meeting sponsored by the Africa Committee, Division of Foreign Missions-National Council of Churches, at San Francisco, California, December 7, 1960, Bishop Lesslie Newbigin clearly gave the African viewpoint. This was just after his study tour of Africa. Young missionaries were saying, "We are the temporary people. We are here to help the African to stand on his own feet, then we shall go . . . We are merely the scaffolding. You are the building. We are temporary. You are permanent." But African leaders said, "If this is the understanding of your task, it is better that you go now rather than later. We are not interested in an African Church. We are interested in a Christian church in Africa, and we regard you as part of the church. . . We want the missionary who will come here, live with us, work with us, die with us, and lay his bones here in Africa."

This whole question involves identification. An African spoke to Newbigin about identification. He said there are two kinds. "One is the anthropological conception of identification; the other is identification in Christ. It is the second in which we are interested."

Is the view of younger churches valid? Yes! This principle of interaction and interrelationship must be used in all human relationships if there is to be peace and progress. Separation of people is wrong. Walls dividing people into black and white, rich and poor, East and West are unchristian. This is sin. It is pride and selfishness that makes us want to keep aloof from people.

We hear about India for the Indians, China for the Chinese, Africa for the Africans, England for the English. This is no more valid than for America to say, America for the Europeans. Separation of people into races and classes breeds hatred and war.

Problems involved in integration of mission and church are very great indeed. There are deep feelings of mistrust, jealousy, and resentments to be overcome. Both missionaries and nationals have problems in working out integration. Let me suggest that a key word in working it out is *forgiveness*. Newbigin says, "Forgiveness is a very costly and difficult process." Church-mission problems must be worked out by sitting down together in Bible study and prayer. The problems of church-mission are more spiritual than they are organizational. And therefore must be worked out in spiritual fellowship.[1]

The central emphasis in the first paragraph of this presentation is fairly plain. The national church takes over the full administration of the program including both church functions and mission activities. Missionaries who are prepared to stay on under the program are so identified with it that they are subject to the direction of the national church administrators in their own mission activities. The main contact by the missionary with the "home" mission board likely would be the receipt of finances for missionary support. All other controls including receipt and disposition of foreign funds would be in the hands of the national church.

The inherent problems in this are at least twofold: (1) To what extent can a foreign mission body corporately or its missionary agent individually subject itself or himself to the

---

[1] Edwin I. Weaver, "The Ministry of Reconciliation in Africa or Bridges of Forgiveness, Love, and Fellowship," a message at the Limuru Study Conference, Limuru, Kenya, March 28-April 1, 1962.

strictures which such national control could impose? Should
the national church lose the vision of the regions beyond,
would such administrative stricture hamstring the evangelistic outreach of the parent missionary body or its workers?
(2) To what extent should a parent church go on giving
funds in an unrestricted way to the national church without
at least being frank and fair in maintaining ultimate control
at least of the mission workers who may be in association
with the national church? Is there not less danger of misunderstanding by effecting a clearcut division of lines of
authority and spheres of cooperation between the parent
mission body and the national church?

C. *Dual Supervision—Church and Mission*

These queries pertaining to the second pattern lead on to
the third pattern of thinking, namely, the pattern of dual
administrative development.

To illustrate the point we take a case example of a mission
body with a field executive committee composed entirely of
missionaries. National leaders participate in the delibera-
tions of the executive only in matters pertaining to indigenous church life. Practically all of the other administrative
functions are performed by mission committees and super-
intendents.

The nationals work in assistant positions but not in top executive posts. With the development of the church and the
rise of the nationalistic spirit, church leaders ask for a greater
voice in mission executive councils. The question is referred
to a home foreign mission board who decide by policy direc-
tive that a dual system of administration shall be developed
involving (a) church administration and (b) mission administration. For the former a central authority is established
with a preponderance of national leaders over mission leaders in the church executive membership. For the latter, distinctly "missions" affairs, such as educational and medical

programs as well as the direction of missionaries, are kept under mission executive control. The view is that until there are national leaders (a) of equivalent spiritual, educational and theological training and experience, and (b) with the same spirit of consecration as missionaries have, no one sees how such national church leaders can be brought into distinctly missions executive administration.

Here is a dual concept—church and missions—with all of the potential of dire misunderstanding between church nationals and mission personnel, with the consequent danger of an outcome divisive in spirit.

D. *Cooperative Partnership*

What is the answer? We propose a dictum which should stand as an axiom in determining the principles of relationship between parent mission bodies and the new national church. It should be understood that neither mission nor church must dominate the other, but both must cooperate as equal partners in their common task.

This is not (1) missionary superintendence or direction alone, (2) national superintendence or direction alone, (3) nor a mere divisive dualism of mission administration and national church organization going their separate paths. This is a coalescence of the best in all three patterns to the point of adequate *cooperation*.

Cooperation! Here mission and the developing church pool their resources of men and money and wisdom and consecration in order to accomplish jointly a job which neither can accomplish alone. Traditionally the mission has been accused of dominating and absorbing the national church until it is a captive church incapable of either self-government or self-support or self-propagation. At the same time the mission has jealously conserved its own independence. Being appointed and supervised by a foreign society, and responsible to that society and the supporting churches for the conduct of their work, missionaries must resist a natural tendency to become sublimely indifferent to the opinions of national Christians and churches. The confident nationalism of today, an increasingly well-trained national leadership, and increasingly mature Christian churches and associations of churches all demand that missionaries cooperate in the work rather than dominate it. National churches maturing into associations of churches *must be taken into partnership.*

This cooperation or partnership has several characteristics. It should be *total* partnership. Although the shared responsibility may be limited at the outset, the partnership eventually must affect all matters of mission activity including policy, finance, administration, and personnel. It should be a *true* partnership. For the mission to invite certain selected individuals into a cooperative relationship on conditions stipulated by the mission is not a satisfactory mission-church relationship, for the foreign missionary is still predominant. Thus when one field recently offered to elect certain individuals to serve in a cooperative capacity in a Bible school program and in the literature program, the home board pointed out that any true partnership between mission and church would permit the national church to choose its own representatives.

Cooperation should develop into *equal* partnership. While *cooperation* may be effected between unequals, *partnership* implies a relationship of equals in a common enterprise. Can national Christian leaders and missionary leaders cooperate as equals? A missionary of a certain society wrote recently of Japanese pastors: "They *are* our equals socially and educationally; in fact, they are superior to us as evangelists and pastors because of their language and their understanding of the Japanese mind." But one might add, they are not our equals financially.

If equal partnership requires that both partners place at the disposal of the partnership *equal amounts of the same assets,* then equal partnership in missions is forever impossible. The national does not have an equal amount of what the missionary has, nor does the missionary have an equal amount of what the national has. The children of this world do seem to be wiser than the children of light. Many a partnership has worked well when one partner put up the money and the other the "know how." A partnership arrangement between capital and labor works out well, for neither has all that is required to do the job, but together they do have what it takes. Neither can say of the other, "I have no need of you." Like husband and wife, they need each other to realize their true potential. So do the mission and the church. Both must pool their equally important but diverse resources of men and money and wisdom and consecration. Having shared their differing but equally vital resources, these partners would share equally in responsibility and authority, administering their joint program by joint boards or a joint council.

Such equal partnership requires the *continuity* of each partner within the partnership. Canon Max Warren, esteemed the world around for the keen insights shared in his Church Mission Society *News-letter*, delivered the Merrick Lectures of 1955 at Ohio Wesleyan University on the subject, "Partnership: the Study of an Idea." After discussing the three essential factors in partnership: involvement, acceptance of responsibility, and acceptance of liability, Warren added:

> Involvement and the acceptance of both responsibility and liability presuppose the continuity within the partnership of each partner. There can be no question of absorption whereby the identity of the partners is lost. The terms of our definition—involvement, responsibility, liability—are meaningless unless this conscious identity of each partner survives.[2]

---

[2] Max Warren, *Partnership: the Study of an Idea* (Chicago: Student Christian Movement Press, 1956), p. 13.

Thus partnership is conditioned upon the continuity of the identity of each partner. Mission and church should not become amalgamated or fused. Neither must absorb the other; although related as equal partners, they must retain their distinct identity. Actually there is some divergence in practice. One African mission reports that it made Africans members of mission committees, amalgamating the mission and the African staff, and placing in their hands the administrative program of both church and mission. Experience, however, seems to indicate the wisdom of maintaining the distinction between mission and church until nationalization is effected. Under this dual arrangement, missionaries organized as a field conference can decide those matters which concern themselves alone (as missionary housing, furlough, missionary children's schooling); and churches organized on a national basis can decide those matters which concern themselves alone. But mission and national church as equal partners and distinct entities should cooperate in planning and implementing the field program which was once considered the prerogative of the mission alone.

E. *Church and Mission Membership*

There are two corollaries established by such a position: (1) During this period of equal partnership, missionaries should identify themselves organizationally with the mission and not with the national church. The line of a missionary's responsibility traces back through his field conference and mission society to the home churches. It is obvious that the interests of the foreign mission and the national church can easily conflict. At such times a foreign missionary could hardly fulfill the obligations of membership in a local church on the field. (2) During this period of equal partnership, nationals should identify themselves organizationally with the national church and not with the foreign mission. They should not be invited to serve as members of mission committees per se. Rather they should be encouraged in the formation of a strong national church administration to which the mission should relate itself in the joint conduct of the work, and to which church body the work can be turned over progressively. Nationals would thus find their normal sphere of service not on a mission committee carrying out the policies and purposes of a foreign mission society, and subject to its supervision. Rather the national should serve on a committee in the context of his own church organization, but cooperating with the missionary on a joint committee.

Thus the national and the missionary should each continue in his own organizational context of church and mission: the permanent and the temporary factors; one responsible to local churches, and the other to a foreign mission society. The mission and church association must be related together as distinct entities and equal partners in their joint work program. When nationalization of the work shall have been effected and the mission organization as such is dissolved, any missionary remaining to serve in any capacity should serve *with* the national church and *under* the national church. It would then be altogether in order for him to identify himself with that church by membership and submit himself to its life and discipline.

Certainly there are obvious difficulties in facing equal partnership in the work. A Brazilian leader wrote:

It demands mutual respect and self-respect. For men of different races to cooperate is not easy. To submit oneself to the domination of the majority is a difficult thing in one's own country, and still more when the majority is of another race and color. To achieve it there become necessary patience, mutual love, confidence, readiness in passing over small differences, in sacrificing minor points of opinion to greater and higher ends, aptness in seeing both sides of questions, and resolute determination to put aside prejudices and suspicions. Because the missionary claims for himself greater Christian experience and richer, perhaps, it behooves him to more fully manifest those gifts.[3]

While problems will certainly arise in implementing a program involving equal partnership with nationals, we must remember that we have had serious problems also in implementing a program involving equal partnership with fellow missionaries! Problems then must not dissuade us. We cannot fight against history. We must be moving in the right direction.

The advantages of such a joint relationship in the work are many:

1. This joint relationship will keep national leaders informed and give them the voice in the program which they have asked for repeatedly.

2. Sharing ideas and counseling together will help break down the barrier between the missionary and the national worker, and teach both to think and work together.

3. Joint study and planning of the work will develop in both the missionary and the national a concern for the whole field.

4. This relationship will secure more friendly cooperation among the churches of the association.

5. Nationals will be afforded the opportunity to get experience in self-government and self-propagation, being thus prepared for the eventual turn-over of the responsibility and authority. After all, the best preparation for leadership is leadership itself.

6. Missionaries will learn several lessons: (a) That they must be willing to accept certain proposals from the national, even if these are considered second best. Our full cooperation in his second-rate program may work out better than his noncooperation in our first-rate (?) program.

---

[3] Joseph R. Woody, *The Brazil Plan of Mission-Church Relations: an Experiment in Partnership* (Richmond, Va.: Union Seminary, 1961), pp. 155-156.

(b) The missionary made some mistakes, too, and learned lessons the hard way, just as the national must. (c) If the nationals should stumble a bit now, the missionary is here to help, whereas if they have no opportunity to stumble until the missionary is out of the picture, there may then be no help and counsel available.

7. It may bring to light real solutions to problems which have baffled our missionaries.

8. It will afford the training program needed by every missionary in training his national counterpart to take increasing responsibility for some particular phase of the work. Without such preparatory training, nationalization can become a farce and a tragedy. Where nationalization has been effected under these procedures, great churches now exist, witnessing effectually for the Lord Jesus Christ.

II. MONEY AND MANPOWER

R. B. Buker, Sr.

A. *Finances*

RECENT WRITERS and speakers have been discussing the subject of the church and missions. There is a definite tendency to blend the two. The church is missions. Missions is the church. Ideologically this has a real basis. It is a very stimulating approach, helping to clarify the significance of the theology and the structure of the application or implementation of the functions of the Christian life and its spread throughout the world.

Realistically, however, it is difficult to develop a program with people as people, with groups of Christians as groups, and with the existing world as we have it if we involve the situation with the present tendency for coalescing until distinctions are lost. We should continue, therefore, at least for the purposes of this study, to consider the sending churches as an entity with a function of missions. This discussion proceeds on this premise.

The Church is the Body of Christ. The main task of the Church is the evangelizing of the world. Our problem is to discover the will of the Holy Spirit in the details for accomplishing the work to be done.

An analysis of the relationship between the sending churches and the field churches, often called the older and the younger churches, provides a basis for determining certain missionary policies and procedures in this area.

Some of the first questions that come to the missionary administrator are in the realm of finances. We are assuming that a group has accepted Jesus Christ and is organized as, or functions in, the capacity of a church. The missionary then must proceed to make some sort of a decision as to the physical relationship between the new church on the field with the mother church or organization from the sending area. Should the sending group assist or subsidize the new group with financial help?

The usual method has been to try to encourage and strengthen a new work by underwriting the material needs of the younger churches. The economic contrast between the sending country and the field where the church is being started is very great. The normal reaction of the average missionary is that we have a moral responsibility to help our weaker brethren at this stage of the work. Every missionary has the expectation that eventually the work will become self-sustaining. The people are poor and become poorer when they become Christians because they jeopardize their former economic position by this strange move. They are but babes in Christ and need time to become strong. Our resources, moreover, are so great in comparison, the obvious thing to do seems to be to assist them to bear their financial burden.

If we grant the soundness of the principle that financial

help from the sending church is justified, can we come to an understanding as to how much help should be given? Should we give all that is involved, or should we give only a part? Usually it is considered wise to provide only a part. If at first all the needs are met by the sending church, then it is only a matter of time before a system of decreasing the help is instituted. The dog's tail is cut off a section at a time.

At this point it should be mentioned that the over-all picture presents some difficulties. Here is a missionary society that seems to have almost unlimited funds. At least it has a great deal to allocate for the paying of national workers and for the erection of buildings. Nearby in the same country there is another missionary group that has limited funds. Since the smaller society is unable to compete on the same basis of money, it faces a serious decision. Should it close its missionary work in that country because of its inability to operate on such a level? We have to consider the reality of the problem. Missionary groups do work in any country on a competitive basis. To a certain degree competition is healthy. When, however, certain methods work toward the elimination of a given group, questions and doubts arise. Is everything being done in accord with the Christian, that is, the New Testament, standard?

It is said that one who will not read history is condemned to commit the mistakes of the past. It would be wise, therefore, to examine what has been done in the past. The Carey, Marshman and Ward triumvirate of the Serampore group in India did sponsor the development of new work around them. It began by providing literature and evangelists. When the first Christians were ready for pastoral supervision, the salary of a national was usually provided by funds from the work at Serampore. We must remember, however, that these funds were not actually foreign as the name usually implies. They were secured by the labors of these three men as they worked in India, teaching, printing, and conducting schools.

The Burma mission was influenced by the philosophy proposed by Adoniram Judson. His intimate knowledge of Buddhism and its methods, particularly the emphasis of the Buddhist priests in urging the people to give and give and give as a matter of merit, thus supporting the Buddhist temples and providing the money for meritorious construction of their pagodas, caused Judson to set the "rule" of asking for *no* money from the early converts. Salvation is free. This basic doctrine must be exemplified by giving them not only the Word but all that was necessary to implement the growing process. The evangelists, the pastors, the church buildings and furniture, all was provided by foreign funds lest the asking for money become a stumbling block to the way of salvation. Offerings or collections were never taken during any of the public meetings from these early Christian groups in Burma.

It would seem that the initial work of the majority of missionary groups has followed substantially the same procedure. The first years of the new church have been helped by the sending church bearing part or all of the financial involvements of the pastor and the erection of a church edifice.

Where the above procedure has not been followed we find what is usually entitled an exception. It will be apropos to cite a few of these exceptions: The Karen work in the Bassein area of Burma was greatly hindered by political persecution. Missionaries Abbott and Carpenter realized that if the work was to go forward, the Christians had to be self-sustaining physically and spiritually. National pastors were ordained and sent forth into the area where no missionaries were permitted. Methods were suggested whereby the Christians developed a sort of "God's acre" in their rice fields and the processing of the rice. The proceeds supported the Christian workers and also provided funds for their churches and schools. This departure from the approved procedures of the established mission, then thirty to forty years old, brought much consternation among the missionaries. Consequently the missionary conference in Burma ostracized these two missionaries. Abbott and Carpenter carried on by faith. The Karen church was able to continue, and developed into the strongest Christian association in Burma. Some years later these missionaries were received back into the Burma Missionary Conference with much honor.

The Lisu work in Yunnan, started by J. O. Fraser of the China Inland Mission, at no time has used foreign funds to subsidize the development of the church in that animistic tribe. The Methodist work in Chile during the last half of the nineteenth century, beginning with self-supporting schools, was able to plant its churches without foreign financial assistance.

Should not New Testament principles be examined to discover what may apply in this area of missionary work? The first question that may be considered is the overall effectiveness of the gospel. Is our gospel unable, when planted, to thrive and grow according to the New Testament pattern of local churches without the aid of external finances even as it did in New Testament times? We realize that God's plan includes the voice of living man as a channel for the gospel message. But does Scripture teach that churches are to be established by the use of foreign funds within a different culture? Historically we know that the gospel within the hearts of men and women was sufficient in the beginning to plant the church in local areas. What then is our reasoning today when we introduce new features to the spread and establishing of local churches? Are we ready to admit that the gospel in itself is not sufficiently effective to accomplish this end as it once did? The illustrations given above indicate that the gospel is still competent to effect its desired results.

Perhaps some would point out that the illustrations given deal with primitive peoples in jungle areas. There are a great number of illustrations that can be given of churches being established in this generation in urban localities with little more than the witness through a human agent that is filled with the Holy Spirit. A group gathers to hear the Word of salvation. With its own resources it acquires property and erects a church. The group maintains normal growth and supports its own pastor. This can be documented in Honolulu, Tokyo, Manila and other cities around the world.

Should not the emphasis be placed upon the scriptural pattern? Does the new church on the field look to humans or God for help and guidance? How does the Holy Spirit guide in such relationships? Is it that the sending societies are directed by Holy Spirit illumination to help the younger churches in this way? Is it possible that Satan will subtly influence the older churches to do those things that seem so right in the beginning but which will weaken the growth and undermine the initiative of the younger growing church? We watch the process of a chicken pecking its way out of its shell. It is so weak certainly we are justified in helping the imprisoned thing by picking off some of the shell. This act of kindness, however, deprives the little chick of that necessary activity which will give it strength to meet life itself. By our act of kindness we cause the death of the chick. Is there a tendency for us to commit a similar disservice in our church planting?

When the indigenous phase of self-government is encouraged on the part of the sending church, the matter of the funds for support of the missionary must be considered. We want the field church to undertake every phase of the church administration as it fulfills the goal of self-government. The missionary is a component of the over-all picture. To be consistent, should not the money for the missionary be sent to the local church government, such as the associational or synodic offices, giving them the responsibility of dispensing these funds along with the other funds of the church activities?

There is also the concept of sharing as we are trying to demonstrate by action as well as by word. We share the plan of salvation. We share our wisdom in matters of doctrines and church policies. To be consistent should we not share in the area of finance? If the older foreign church is of a mind to share in the expense of national workers, should not the dispensing of these funds be entrusted to the church group set up on the new field? And if this is done should not the next step include the finances of the missionaries who are so intimately connected with this section of the work?

If this matter is approached as a business proposition, what would be the answer? Who sets the missionary salary? Would any business set a salary scale in one department and then have it paid from another department? Certainly, this is a regular procedure: The executive branch will decide the salary scale of the various departments and the treasury or accounting department will pay out the money. Does this develop a sense of indigenity on the part of the accounting personnel? No, it does not. The accounting department feels a definite sense of responsibility to the executive. If the home board of the foreign mission society sets the salary of the missionary and then asks a field group of nationals to act as paymaster we cannot expect that this will produce a sense of independence to encourage indigenous attitudes and actions on the part of the field church. It will engender the spirit of dependence upon the foreign sponsors.

The Methodists have worked on this problem for more than a generation in South India. When Indian bishops were appointed the missionaries of the area became subject to the bishopric in every way. All matters of administration including finances were handled through the bishop's office. Sufficient time has elapsed to determine the value of the system in terms of developing an indigenous Methodist church. In general from an outsider's viewpoint we would conclude that this particular phase of the approach to indigenous work has not contributed to its establishment. The attitude generated by the periodic receiving of funds from a foreign source does not encourage firm indigenous procedures. It rather tends to perpetuate a pattern of dependence.

Once again we are faced with the importance of evaluating the results of our efforts as foreigners to share and to identify ourselves with the field church. Is it possible to overdo the matter so that we produce on the part of the young church a feeling of adherence and connection that prevents the free initiative and spontaneity so effective in true indigenous work? Our objective, after we have given them the tools of the doctrine and after they possess the Holy Spirit, is to have them operate by themselves in a true indigenous manner.

This objective, therefore, brings us to the question, Does interchurch aid (from home to field) violate indigenous principles?

We should perhaps subdivide the kinds of aid that the older church may give to the newer church. There is one kind of aid that all would agree is legitimate. This is help in time of special emergency when there is a famine, a flood, a fire, or some such circumstance that results in a temporary need. We have scriptural accounts in Acts where churches helped each other in such situations. It is interesting to note that in Acts it was the new church that helped the old church in Jerusalem. Wherever such need arises, however, all would admit the validity of aid.

There are other kinds of aid which would fall into the category of spiritual assistance which can be given to churches. Nearby churches can provide spiritual encouragement during special meetings. Delegations visiting the church involved provide a spiritual influence that is a real ministry.

"Aid" in the content of this discussion usually refers to financial aid. Regular financial aid from older and foreign churches to the younger and local churches as a regular procedure would definitely violate indigenous principles. It would be introducing a foreign element into the operation of the local church. A letter-of-the-law adherence to any given principle can kill the results. This could be true as we strive to establish the church along indigenous lines. The word "indigenous" in itself is not a sacred cow. However, the objective of a self-sustaining church is extremely important. In the concept of "self-sustaining" are included all the elements of governing, supporting, reproducing—all that would be included in independence but not isolation. It is quite possible that along the road of attaining this goal it would seem wise as a Spirit-guided act to permit certain nonindigenous activity. It is generally agreed that some sort of "priming the pump" may be necessary at the beginning of a particular work. This may be merely the sending of a missionary who is a foreigner to initiate the work. Perhaps it could mean the giving of financial aid for workers, rent, or construction work, and so forth. Historical evidence, however, is producing more and more factual material to show that where there is a will there is a way to develop local churches anywhere in the world without material aid that crosses cultures. The result is a much healthier church that tends to develop into a self-propagating unit within its own environment.

Sometimes the act of sharing or helping in time of special need is confused with indigenous effort. We do want the Christian churches to be able to stand alone, to grow by reason of energy generated by the Holy Spirit. The Holy Spirit may lead the older church to be used in the growth of the new in a different culture. Mainly, however, it is the Word—the living Word—that we break and share with the newer churches. It is significant to note how history reveals that this miracle of a new church and its growth is accomplished with a minimum of material factors using just the Word as the dynamic for the complete operation.

B. *Organizations*

Church relationships anywhere in the world require a consideration of interchurch organizations. A few local groups try to continue an existence of isolation. This, however, is not a satisfactory situation. Several factors bring strong pressure upon Protestant Christians until they are forced to examine the ways whereby some sort of relatedness may be evolved to answer the needs. How can Protestantism achieve a united voice in a world where influence and strength of religious position are important? We have a goal and responsibility to spread our message among two billion people who do not know our gospel of salvation. United we stand, divided we fall. How can we present a united front for this task? How can we best deploy our forces to accomplish our purposes? These and similar questions have prodded Protestant Christians in the first half of the twentieth century to initiate movements which have resulted in ecumenical activity in terms of Christian councils and international committees. Milestones along the road of ecumenical history are Edinburgh in 1910, which produced in due time the International Missionary Council that met in Jerusalem in 1928, Tambaram, Madras in 1938, Whitby in 1947 and Ghana in 1959. This particular unit was swallowed up in the World Christian Council at New Delhi in 1961. The World Council of Churches was organized in Utrecht, Holland in 1938. From time to time it has met and strengthened its organization and its procedures.

After more than a quarter of a century we are now able to evaluate the trends of this ecumenical movement within the Protestant churches. The men who sponsored and led the various divisions of this over-all operation at the beginning were men of vision and conviction. They had a passion to do a great work for the Lord. Gradually, however, the potential dangers inherent in such a program became evident. The organization became more and more hierarchical. This has ever been declared a principle but the actual manifestation of its procedures indicates this. More and more groups who wished for spiritual fellowship and encouragement found themselves within a framework that was dominated by centralization.

Doctrinally this large structure seemed to have a statement that was satisfactory to evangelicals. Soon, however, it became evident that denominations with liberal theological orientation found an active place in the World Council. In fact it seems that men with a definite liberal theological position naturally gravitated to positions of leadership. This is not acceptable to evangelicals.

Groups with conservative theological orientation find themselves in a dilemma. It is recognized that Christians should work together. But to work with and under liberals is not logical or desirable. The obvious solution is that evangelicals should group together in order to function as a unit. Having agreed upon this step, the nature of the organization must be decided.

Should evangelicals pattern their organization after that of the World Council? Given an acceptable doctrinal basis, should they unite on a council basis? Realizing the tendency for a hierarchy to develop through the councils, it would seem wiser to work through associations which would preserve a stronger emphasis on fellowship rather than organization. If these can be developed on national levels, the success achieved in smaller units would serve as a norm for an international organization. The lessons learned from the past should serve as guideposts to a more satisfactory organism for the future.

Another question that faces evangelicals is in the area of denominations. How elaborately and extensively should denominations try to organize? It has been quite evident that denominations do well to organize on a national level. There is much that can be done effectively only when the churches move and act together. A major area where this is demon-

strated is missions. If each church were to be a missionar
society independent of other churches, practically nothin
could be accomplished. When the churches of a denomina
tion unite to form a sending society, many missionaries ca
be sent to many lands with a commendable procedure fo
all. There are many other activities that would illustrate thi

The next consideration in connection with denomination
is whether there should be international alliances for th
separate denominations. There are reasons why this is de
sirable. The interchange and sharing that come through suc
an alliance will strengthen the work of the national unit
Work for extension of the Lord's vineyard to unevangelize
areas can be equitably shared on a comity basis.

There is one consideration in connection with denomina
tions that might act as a precaution in the promotion of de
nominational alliances in countries where the new churche
are being established. It is a common statement among lead
ers of the younger churches that denominations are impose
upon them as elements of Western culture. They do not un
derstand them too well and in general if the Westerner wer
removed the denomination itself would disappear or at leas
be greatly deemphasized. The first reaction to this would b
to encourage the denominational leaders not to stress th
individuality of any given denomination. It may have serve
as a vehicle to bring the gospel to a given people but it nee
not be perpetuated.

A more careful analysis of people (of every race and lan
guage) and their reactions all over the world leads us t
realize that diversification into groups is a normal matte
The Buddhists, the Muslims, the Hindus, and the Roma
Catholics all have a great many divisions within themselve
It is not exceptional that Protestants should be afflicted wit
the same weakness. It is a human trait. If it were possib
to abolish all denominations in a country such as Africa o
Asia and to leave the Christians of that country completel
free of Western leadership over a given period of time, ther

is no doubt that the Christians of that country would in due process of time develop divisions of their own.

It is probably true that Asiatics or Africans would not develop the same kind of denominations as we now find in Europe and America. In behalf of self-determination, therefore, it may be unwise to impose the Western denominations upon other lands any longer than is necessary to plant Christianity (local churches) in a given culture.

In the light of this situation it may be desirable that Christians around the world should sponsor conservative evangelical interdenominational associations or fellowships rather than world alliances of different denominations. This would permit the younger churches to develop along indigenous patterns fitted to their own cultures. Each country can well have its own local group fellowships that do not expect to cross cultural barriers. Jesus Christ is supracultural and supradenominational. Internationally we present Him as the common unifying center.

Hubert Reynhout, Jr.

There is cause for serious concern for the current Christian missionary situation. All is not well; in fact, almost everything is in a state of crisis, and almost everyone is confused. We are confronted with the resurgence of indigenous religions in mission field countries, with a tidal wave of worldwide nationalism and frequent anti-American and antimissionary feelings, and with the wildfire growth of Communism. We must consider "the missionary implications of the end of Western colonialism and the collapse of Western Christendom." [4] Although the world "Christian" community has grown during the past centuries, until today "about 8 percent of the world's population . . . is Protestant, 17 percent is Roman Catholic, and 5 percent is Ortho-

---

[4] Source of quotation unknown.

dox and ancient Eastern—a total of 30 percent," yet "if present rates of growth in world population and in the 'Christian' community continue, the proportion by the year 2,000 A.D. may be 20 percent, and Protestants may be only 5 percent of the people on our globe." [5]

Such conditions and possibilities necessitate an honest and thorough Biblical appraisal of world missions. Previous articles have considered *why* the church should engage in missions, *what* the objectives should be, and *who* should be involved in the work. The problem of this section is the crucial practical one: *how* should the missionary enterprise be directed and carried on? This brings us immediately to questions of church relationships and their bearing on the missionary ministry and the fulfillment of the Great Commission. We face and need to overcome, if possible, the criticism that "by and large, missions are conceived and performed (without knowing or intending it) in an amateurish way." [6] The fact that a work is God's work and can only be successful as He blesses it is no excuse for our doing less than our very human best!

This analysis of church relationships will scrutinize the three critical areas of personnel, finances, and organizations, attempting to set forth for each first, certain Biblical principles, followed by desirable or possible modern applications. Two thousand years separate our age from New Testament times, and it is not at all certain just what Jesus would be saying and doing if He were living in our day, or just how Paul and the other disciples would practice the Christian life and propagate the Christian faith. Perhaps, however, some

---

[5] Frank Wilson Price, "Ecumenical Streams in Protestant Christianity," *Occasional Bulletin* from the Missionary Research Library, XI, No. 4 (April 30, 1960), 3.

[6] Hendrick Kraemer, "Syncretism as a Theological Problem for Missions," a chapter in *The Theology of the Christian Mission*, edited by Gerald H. Anderson (New York: McGraw-Hill Book Company, Inc., 1961), pp. 179-182.

guide lines may be seen and present-day applications drawn out.

A. *Questions of Personnel*

Very much of the success of the work of the church and of missions depends upon people. This is not only true humanly speaking, but also from God's point of view. The record of the early spread of the gospel emphasizes, of course, the work of God the Holy Spirit. But He used people: there would have been no witness and no Church without Peter and Paul and James and John and scores of other such dedicated men and women. "Ye are the light of the world. . . . Ye are the branches. . . . Ye shall be witnesses unto me," and many more truths support this idea. In a sense, God Himself does the work; in another sense, the work is not and cannot be done without proper personnel.

1. Biblical Principles. There seem to be two outstanding Biblical principles relating to the personnel used of God in the proclamation of the gospel and the propagation of the church:—

First, there should be some carefully chosen professional missionaries. Christ chose twelve to accompany Him and to learn from Him, whom He appointed to represent Him and to preach the Word of God after His ascension. "Upon this rock," He said, "I will build my church" (Matt. 16:18). Then Paul was an especially chosen minister to reach the Gentiles. Paul himself selected several, his "sons in the faith," whom he faithfully taught and finally ordained to a spiritual apostolate. Occasionally we find others, too, raised up of God and approved by the church leaders for the Christian ministry, like Priscilla and Aquilla and Apollos. These examples suffice to illustrate the Biblical principle of there being carefully chosen professional missionaries, whose chief duty it was to devote themselves to the ministry.

Second, every church member, every single Christian,

should become a lay witness to Jesus Christ. The injunction for spiritual service was upon all. They who were scattered abroad by persecution went everywhere preaching the Word. It is the clear consensus of opinion that the command of Christ to witness was—and still is—incumbent upon every Christian. Special gifts for special services were given to a few, but the privilege and responsibility of bearing testimony to His saving grace was equally upon all. "Christian laymen must recognize their responsibility for the evangelization of the world. . . . Every child of God . . . is to be a witness for Christ, witnessing with his life as well as by word of mouth. . . . 'There are many contrasts between current Christianity and that of Christ's day, but the limitation of the ministry to a professional class of men is the most shocking of all these contrasts.'" [7]

2. Modern Applications. Missionary service today, more than ever, should be recognized as a highly specialized profession. This is a day and age of specialization. Not everyone can be a physician, nor even a veterinarian, nor even a mechanic or farmer! Each vocation, to be successfully entered and practiced, requires specialized talents and preparation. This is certainly true for missionary work.

The missionary faces needs and problems, opportunities and responsibilities that demand unique knowledge and ability for fulfillment. Christian experience and character, spiritual maturity, thorough learning in the Scriptures and theology, practice in church affairs, empathetic understanding of other people, other cultures and religions and ways of life, professional education in missionology—these are all priorities for missionary candidates.

Today's missionaries need to be people who have overcome provincialism and sectarianism, who can work with and both lead and follow congenially and even enthusiastically people of other countries and colors. There is no need

---

[7] T. B. Maston, *Christianity and World Issues* (New York: The Macmillan Company, 1957), pp. 342, 345.

for personal or racial or denominational pride or distinction in the modern missionary movement; these will hurt rather than help our cause.

The Church of Jesus Christ should be represented especially in missions by her best—most gifted—members. This has not always been the case. There should be a sympathetic but emphatic rejection of candidates who are not personally and professionally equipped to do the missionary task assigned to them with both zeal and knowledge. Whatever the special duty of a missionary—evangelism, medicine, education, literature, radio, or any phase of any of these—his being a missionary, representing the Lord Jesus Christ and His Church, is his first major, and must receive adequate preparation and attention.

Since the success of the gospel in all the world is so directly related to the professional personnel who serve the gospel, this is the first consideration of the Church in her missionary task.

In addition, however, we must underscore both the multiplied opportunities and responsibilities which lay witnessing has in our modern world. True Christian people are a minority even in our own country and rub shoulders with nominal Christians or unbelievers in all walks of life. Wherever there is a Christian, there should be a gospel light shining. There is no hope for total world evangelism that will somehow touch every human being—and this is the command of Christ —unless every Christian in every country gets under the burden of witnessing for Christ. The Church should be actively stimulating and training her members for day-by-day witnessing in the highways and byways. Work for Christ is not the special prerogative of a few, but the divine imperative for all!

These emphases: carefully chosen professional missionaries for specialized tasks, and all-member dedication for general lay witnessing, seem to be the only combination that is both scripturally ordained and presently apt to succeed.

B. *Questions of Finances*

While nothing can be done without proper personnel, little can be done well without sufficient funds. Money is a universal need. Missions, though a divine calling, is also largely dependent upon monetary aid to be effectively carried out. This has always been true, though there were times when individuals simply provided for themselves and received little aid from other Christians or churches. That possibility still exists for some who will serve as part-time missionaries abroad, supporting themselves in business or government employ. But it is jeopardizing the life of missions itself to depend on such service today. According to sound estimates, Protestant missions last year with over 40,000 missionaries and their many great avenues of service were supported by about $200,000,000. If missions are to minister successfully in the immediate future, much more money must be poured into them. But the giving and receiving of money raises questions which we must seek to answer.

1. Biblical Principles. The New Testament Scriptures have a great deal to say about finances, and some of it bears on the missionary outreach of that first century. Apart from such general principles as: "It is more blessed to give than to receive," "the laborer is worthy of his hire," and "the love of money is the root of all evil"—all of which bespeak an important message to the church and the Christian—there are two other Biblical principles that we should examine for guidance in our modern missionary enterprise.

First, money was collected by the apostolic church to meet very definite needs. The first church collection of which we read is that in Acts 4, 5, and 6. The Jerusalem church established a communal life; "neither said any of them that aught of the things which he possessed was his own; but they had all things common." Those that had possessions sold them and pooled the funds, "and distribution was made unto every man according as he had need." Eventually "seven men of honest report, full of the Holy Ghost and wisdom" were appointed over this business. Apparently these needs were primarily the physical and material needs of Christian converts. The second church collection is that most fully described in II Corinthians 8 and 9, a collection the Apostle Paul exhorted of the churches on his third missionary journey as he was returning to Jerusalem, to be used to help the poor saints there in their penury. This, too, was for material needs. In addition we do find Paul and the other missionaries receiving occasional financial remuneration from those whom they had benefited, and of this Paul wrote, "Ye have well done, that ye did communicate with my affliction" (Phil. 4:14).

Second, money collected was usually distributed by the local church or duly appointed representatives. In the collections of Acts 4, 5, and 6, the gifts were "laid down at the apostles' feet," who themselves first saw to the distribution, but who later were replaced by the first seven deacons, whom "the whole multitude [of Christians] chose." As regards Paul's collection for the saints in Jerusalem, we do not read anything of just what was done with the money nor of who did it, nor how. But we may conjecture from other examples that Paul would give the money to the church for her care and distribution. After all, he appealed to the church assembly for judgment concerning the treatment of Gentile converts (Acts 15), and on his reaching Jerusalem on return from his third missionary journey, we read that "the brethren received [them] gladly," and "the day following" when "all the elders were present, . . . he declared particularly what things God had wrought among the Gentiles by his ministry" (Acts 21). So the local church receives the money collected from abroad and is presumably made the party responsible for its distribution.

2. Modern Applications. There is not very much to go on in these New Testament cases for application to our very highly involved modern missionary financial structure. But perhaps there is enough.

In the first place, all Christians, regardless of race, country, color, or station in society are brethren and are to bear one another's burdens. If a Christian community in Timbuktu has a definite need—it may be medical or material or educational—a need which they cannot meet by themselves, then it is scriptural and proper to help them by financial gifts from other Christians and churches, whether nearby or abroad. In fact, we may say (see II Corinthians 8 and 9) that it would be quite improper and unchristian not to help them. Interchristian or interchurch aid of this kind by itself neither abets nor abrogates indigenous principles, but it does fulfill other principles. In any case, "indigenous" should never mean isolated; no group of Christians is to be fully removed from the rest of the Church. It seems to be immaterial what the origin of the money which serves the Church as long as it helps her when and where she cannot help herself. Of course, no money is to be given that will violate the spiritual life and growth of a church, and no money is to be given "that other men be eased, and ye burdened" (II Cor. 8:13). Insofar as is humanly possible, each person—and each church—should be financially self-sufficient. When this is not possible, we are to help provide for one another.

The principle that I have stated, and would underscore, is that such financial aid of one church to another is *to help a needy church when and where she cannot help herself.* Such help is to be true help and no hurt at all. All of this only reliable and experienced missionary personnel can correctly determine.

We must not think such help to be for material, physical, and educational needs only, but also for evangelistic and spiritual needs. The needs may as often be for men and equipment as for money per se. We do envisage a church responsible to evangelize her own area and countrymen. But many of the younger churches are so small and struggling that their needs for help from Christians and churches outside in the basic task of evangelism are very great indeed, and as much if not more in basic spiritual instruction of new believers. In fact, this was one of the first missionary services of Saul (later Paul) when he was called from Tarsus by the Antioch church to bring them much needed spiritual instruction (Acts 11).

The total duty of the church includes meeting as much as possible all the needs of all people, with emphasis on the spiritual needs first of all. According to the Great Commission, evangelizing, converting, planting church fellowships, and Christian instruction are the primary missionary responsibilities. Wherever these are lacking, there is a mission field. The Christian and the church anywhere are in some measure responsible for this missionary task everywhere. A church's resources in both men and money are to be dedicated to this end, and are to be made available where the need is greatest. The degree of support from the home church to a field church is to be governed primarily by the degree of need.

The problem of channeling, controlling, and using the finances given by one church to another from one country to another is on the face of it quite simple, as we have seen from the Pauline example. If there is a semblance of a local church in a mission field for which missionary money is being given, it can be and should be placed at the disposal of this young church, earmarked for needs if advisable, with such control and such counsel from missionaries as is sensible in the situation.

We know of course that the apparent simplicity of financing missions through local mission field churches is only superficial, and that in the actual processes of handling money there is compounded complexity. Especially in this modern day of expensive missionary means—literature, radio, use of aircraft, medical and educational institutions—is the missionary financial picture complicated. For missions today is big business! Nevertheless, as rapidly as possible the home and sending churches must trust the young mission field churches to handle the funds correctly and honestly. The young churches must prove themselves worthy of such trust, or the funds will properly be cut off or channeled otherwise. There must be a great deal of communication, consultation, and cooperation in these delicate matters. When practical experiences seem to sour us on the simple scriptural principles, let us keep two things at least in mind: that Christ entrusted Judas with the bag even though he was a thief! and that the stewardship of money is a necessary character test.

These emphases: that money is meant to meet spiritual and human needs, and that the church of the locality (where there is a church) should have the major responsibility for its fair distribution, seem to be the scriptural and practical answers to the missionary problems revolving about inter-church (home to field) financial aid.

C. *Questions of Organizations*

Like personnel and money, organization in principle seems almost a *sine qua non* to modern missions. Individual enthusiasts once may have worked alone. Some may still be trying to. But one gets the feeling that individualized and isolated efforts in missions, be they ever so noble, are very feeble and eventually are doomed to fail. This is a day of big organizations—big businesses, big governments, united efforts, combines—and the little man who operates independently, be he in secular or spiritual service, is being squeezed out of existence. We may try to resist the trend; it may be kicking at the pricks! What are some scriptural principles of church or missionary organization, and how may we make modern application of them in the times in which we live for God's glory?

1. Biblical Principles. Organization is indigenous to the

Bible. The Israelites of the Old Testament were a closely knit organization, a nation under judges or kings. The Church of the New Testament was conceived, not so much as a physical organization as a *spiritual* organism: primarily as the Bride of Christ, His Body, the living temple of the Holy Spirit. And yet we do see some organizational germs which may guide us in making or using missionary organizations today.

First, there seems to be in New Testament times just one church fellowship in any one locality. There was one church or Christian group in Corinth, and Philippi, and elsewhere. In fact, the Apostle Paul severely rebukes the Corinthians for creating divisions within the group, which were "of Paul . . . of Apollos . . . of Cephas . . . of Christ." This, he says, is evidence of their carnality! The apostle exhorts estranged Christians in Philippi "that they be of the same mind in the Lord." One wonders what Paul would write to our divided Protestantism today! His own efforts were to keep together fellow Christians—even to honor honest differences of opinion, as long as they did not violate basic truths. Contemplate how he brought his problem of Gentile converts and the law of Moses to the council in Jerusalem, and sought their counsel and consensus!

Second, local Christian fellowships were made to understand their common universal Christian fellowship as much as possible, as seen at the council in Jerusalem, Paul and Barnabas representing the church of Antioch. Paul in his letters speaks of the church fellowship in one place to that of another, passes on the greetings of the Christians, commends the members of one church in their sojourning to the members of another church, and seeks to establish mutual intercommunication. Of course, he also warns of false teachers and pseudo brethren who would deceive for personal advantage, and stresses the sound doctrines of the faith and the true evidences of the spiritual life. But the weight of his influence was to bring Christians to a more profound understanding of the oneness of the Christian fellowship and their enjoyment of the same.

2. Modern Applications. We have today nearly 2,000 years of church history behind us, and a disunited church solidly crystalized and highly organized in manifold divisions. All of them help confuse the missionary picture and compound the missionary problems. What is a serious convert, desiring to enter the true fellowship of the saints and to find doctrinal soundness, to do? Five hundred groups may give five hundred different, even mutually contradictory, answers! In this fogged-up situation we also have many evidences of deep desires to break through these inherited encrustations of the past, and to effect some kind of church unity in our world and in our time. Various regional or national associations or councils of Christians and churches are formed and thriving. Some presume to represent and speak for a majority of Protestants: the national Christian councils. Ecumenicity is growing. There are also small and protesting groups of Christians; some are extremely sectarian. These confuse other attempts to clarify the picture. What are we to think?

Let us at least try to draw up certain conclusions: Local or national or international church organizations are not the God-given answer to the missionary problems of our times per se, but some kind of national and international interchristian and interchurch fellowship—a loose and cooperative kind of organization—seems both scripturally sound and practically necessary to make any genuine spiritual Christian impact in or upon our modern world. "United we stand; divided we fall" was never more true than today. It is futile for us to preach peace and brotherhood—which are certainly elements of the gospel—if we do not have or want both peace and brotherhood with fellow though differing Christians!

We must stand unabashed for the faith once for all delivered to the saints but at the same time we need to minimize our denominational and doctrinal differences. Let us not compromise on fundamentals, but let us not make major issues out of minor! Some would make mode of baptism a supreme issue, others the exact manner of the Lord's return. Too often the sacraments (ordinances) divide whereas they ought to unite. Such misplaced emphases deserve the rebuke of Paul and the more moderate judgment of the first council of Jerusalem. Those who have actual missionary field experience can recite many instances of wonderful interfellowship in spite of wide differences, and the sad curtailing of that very fellowship once back home and bolstered by denominationalism. Brethren, such things ought not so to be—at home, any more than abroad.

We need to recognize that there is much more room in the Christian fellowship for differing and conflicting ideas and practices than we are wont to allow! Our narrow little cliques are not the church. The church has both Mary and Martha, both Paul and Peter, both Onesimus and Philemon, both mystical John and doubting Thomas, both wise, noble, and mighty and foolish, weak, and base. Let us not despise nor jump to criticize our honest differences. Doctrinal purity is not determined by minor issues, but by those of major import. And, as important as doctrinal purity is, it is not the *summum bonum* of Christianity. Love is that! And love is the most lacking of all Christian blessings.

The answer, in part, to our critical missionary problems today is found in Christians getting together, in loose fellowship at least, a fellowship that crosses national and denominational boundaries. Yes, we need national councils of churches, interdenominational alliances, a world council of churches, and a world evangelical fellowship. These various associations and fellowships too should be drawn together, so that the world Christian community may be one. We do not need or want a world superchurch organization, but we do need a universal Christian fellowship that allows for differences within the common true faith. We need to see ecumenical relations fostered. We need to seek to live in spiritual fellowship with all the Christian brethren. But without any fatal compromise. We need again and afresh to most carefully and most sensibly think through our Christian theology and heroically act on what we are led to accept as basic Biblical principles. Christian missions—Christian survival—today more than ever demands this kind of appraisal.

III. *ECUMENICAL SPIRIT*

Arthur M. Climenhaga

THE GREAT MOVEMENT of the Christian church in the world today is toward unity. Organization and union seem almost to be the *sine qua non* in modern church life. This is the day of big enterprise and the little program which operates independently, in secular or spiritual service, is in danger of being squeezed out of existence. Individual groups may once have worked alone; but one gets the feeling that individualized and isolated efforts in churches, be they ever so noble, eventually are doomed to fail unless they operate in the context of some sort of larger unity. They may try to resist the trend, but can they succeed?

Thus the considerations before us have to do with (a) the scriptural principles of church organization and spiritual unity, (b) the development of the same into modern ecumenical movements, and (c) an assessment in the light of these considerations as to the direction for evangelical bodies, particularly in the younger and new church areas (mission fields), to consider in observing Christ's command to unity while at the same time avoiding the pitfalls of modern ecumenicalism.

A. *Organization and Spiritual Unity*

Briefly stated, organization and spiritual unity are particularly indigenous to the Bible. The Israelites of the Old Testament were a closely knit organization, whether as a composite of tribes in a federal sense under the judges or as a more or less organic unity under kings. The Church of the New Testament was conceived not so much as a physical organization as a spiritual organism, primarily as the Body of Christ, the living temple of the Holy Spirit. Yet we do see some organizational germs which may guide us in thinking of interchurch relationships today.

In New Testament times there was apparently just one church fellowship in each locality; however, there was evidently a simple relationship among the churches one with another. There was also a recognition of the importance of fostering unity of doctrine through consultation with the brethren in Jerusalem.

But what do we see today in the development of organization toward unity? We are increasingly able after more than a quarter of a century to evaluate trends in the ecumenical movement within the Protestant and Orthodox churches.

B. *Development of Ecumenical Movement*

As first, this large structure apparently had a statement that was doctrinally satisfactory to those who accepted the authority of the Bible as the Word of God. Certain leaders in the developing ecumenical movement spoke forthrightly for ecumenicity in evangelical tones and patterns. To a point this is to be seen even today as, for instance, in the writings of one of the outstanding ecumenical leaders who states:

> It is not that we are called to unity for our own sakes, by the almost desperate situation of the Church in the world; we are called to it for the sake of Christ, the ful-

fillment of whose good purpose for His world is constantly being frustrated by the division in His Church.[8]

However, despite the evangelical aura of certain outstanding leaders in the ecumenical movement, which ultimately became the World Council of Churches, it became evident that denominations and leaders oriented toward the liberal and humanistic theological positions seemed to gravitate rather naturally into major positions of leadership. This became a grave problem to many Evangelicals and to some this development was entirely unacceptable.

Thus groups oriented toward conservative theological positions found themselves in a dilemma. It was recognized that Christians should work together. But to work in total unity with theological liberals or doctrinal humanists was not only difficult—to many it was totally unacceptable. Finally it became quite evident that not all church bodies, mission organizations and other segments of Christendom could agree to the call to ecumenicity, at least in the terms in which it was presented. Nor could they feel the sharp necessity of unity as spelled out by the ecumenical movements. It should be emphasized that this was due more to reservations on the matter of doctrine than that of polity alone. Back in 1942, Dorothy L. Sayers so aptly observed in the January *International Review of Missions:*

> That there is a great split today in Christendom nobody would deny; but the line of the cleavage does not run between Catholic and Protestant or between Conformist and Nonconformist. It runs, as it ran sixteen centuries ago, between Arius and Athanasius—between those who believe that salvation is of God and those who believe that salvation is of man.[9]

---

8 Bishop Stephen Neill, *The Unfinished Task* (New York: Friendship Press, n.d.), p. 204 ff.

9 Quoted from Samuel Zwemer's *Evangelism Today,* (New York: Fleming H. Revell Co., 1944).

Consequently, hand in hand with the development of federal unity moving into the hierarchical unity as apparently expressed in the evolution of the World Council of Churches, we have seen the counter- or codevelopment of other bodies involving international, intranational, denominational, and interdenominational alliances, amalgamations, and/or fellowships. Tragically, some of these movements have manifested a fighting and divisive spirit both in Western homeland churches and more tragically in young churches on the mission fields. One could document by name and place an internecine development in an Oriental setting where a certain organization came in and in the name of orthodoxy and a stated spirit of twentieth-century reformation split wide open an existent strong, theologically conservative church. Thus we have the dilemma of ultraliberalism and ultrafundamentalism muddying the waters of interchurch organization and cooperation.

C. *Evangelicals Facing Modern Trends*

What then is the answer for churches and groups which as thoroughgoing evangelicals wish to observe the Biblical command for unity (John 17) and yet earnestly contend for the faith (Jude, v. 3) when it relates to the problem of interchurch participation and relationships? On one hand in the context of their evangelical heritage these churches are oriented to a theologically conservative position which can be legitimately divisive; on the other they recognize the validity of the call to the unity of the Spirit in the Apostle Paul's writing and to the unity of believers as expressed in our Lord's high-priestly prayer (John 17).

We hear the ecumenical position stated thus:

> The first thing which is evident is that all our thinking today must be ecumenical. In the political field we are painfully aware that we live in one world. An event in some distant part of the world may set our house

aflame. Economic dislocation in another country may send our economy reeling. We have not quite so clearly realized this in the affairs of the Church. But such great events as the Evanston Assembly of the World Council of Churches in 1954 have brought home to innumerable people the interdependence of the Churches, and the real unity of life and purpose which underlies their many divisions.

The churches need to be converted on the subject of division and unity. It is a commonplace that the aim of the ecumenical movement is the unity and renewal of the Church. It is equally a commonplace that the call for Church union is coming most strongly from the lands of the younger churches. It is certainly not the case that Church union is among the primary interests of churches in the Western world.

What is the situation of the Church today? We look out on disobedient churches and an unfinished task. What of the past? It can be summed up in two phrases. It is the history of disobedient churches and of an unfinished task. And yet God has used even those disobedient churches to do great things, and has brought into being a universal Church.[10]

From the vantage point of our particular and peculiar evangelical heritage with its great dual emphasis on cooperation with all the saints wherever they may be found and "coming out from among" those who are recreant to the faith, we are constrained to wonder how far we should go both in participation and in opposition to the above views. Are there legitimate areas where young churches and missions can cooperate on a neutral plane with churches not measuring up to the same standards of evangelical or conservative Biblical belief without vitiating standards? Can broad interchurch relationships without regard to differing theological positions be maintained on local or territorial

---

[10] Neill, *op. cit.*, pp. 201, 203 ff., 221 ff.

levels by avoiding organic association with larger ecumenical units? Should this break down with a move of a section of the organization toward affiliation or even amenability to a world ecumenical movement (e.g., World Council of Churches) or to a regional or continental movement (e.g., All Africa Church Conference)? What should the evangelical bodies in the local organization consider doing? Are there any basic principles to be adduced to this out of experience? Where do we go in drawing our conclusions?

1. *Intermission and Interdenominational Conferences*

A personal answer to these questions comes out of the writer's experience in administrative work and associations on the mission field in southern Africa.[11] Early in the mission program in various parts of southern Africa about the turn of the century the European missionaries formed bodies known as missionary conferences. These conferences to all intents and purposes were associations for the particular purpose of a united voice in representations to be made to governments—in a sense they were mission guilds and dealt largely with sociopolitical and educational considerations. Only latterly did they also begin to bend toward more definitive theological and allied ethical considerations. Then too in the course of time indigenous or national workers formed African missionary conferences under the tutelage of the parent bodies to consider the same question from an indigenous perspective. In Southern Rhodesia, in 1954, these two bodies were amalgamated into a multiracial Christian council of churches and missions known as the Southern Rhodesia Christian Conference. The writer was elected as the first president and served three two-year terms up to 1960.

The Southern Rhodesia Christian Conference comprised eighteen denominations, societies, and agencies—a cross-

---

11 The writer was general superintendent from 1951-1960 of the Brethren in Christ Church Mission, Southern and Northern Rhodesia, Africa.

cut of sacerdotal, conformist and ultracongregationalist churches, nondenominational faith missions, and the British and Foreign Bible Society; a crosscut as well of various theological perspectives (e.g., Calvinistic and Arminian)—not interfering with each other's Biblical understandings or church polity, but united in prosecuting the work for the Lord Jesus Christ and His kingdom.

When the writer became president of the SRCC in 1954, the conference had no affiliation as a body with any ecumenical groups. While the conference through its secretariat maintained fraternal relations with certain extraterritorial organizations, no organic affiliations were allowed in consideration of those who for theological polity reasons were opposed to certain types of ecumenical connections of the liberal type. Several member churches or missions frankly stated that, were any affiliation to be effected with either the World Council of Churches or the International Missionary Council, they would have to review their membership position in light of positions taken by home boards of control or by supporting constituencies. It was evident that this could lead to withdrawals from the conference. The writer and his home Board for World Missions were among those who felt this way.

However, the pressure from certain of the larger conference denominational members for some sort of affiliation on the part of the Conference with IMC or WCC became stronger especially from 1958 to 1960.[12] Also a more vocal and forceful presentation by certain leading churchmen for church union or unions was manifest and finally came to a climax in an address delivered at the 1960 SRCC conference on the subject, "The Reconciling Witness of the Church Through Church Union." The speaker began by expressing

---

12 Recent correspondence to the writer (August, 1962) from a mission administrator in the Rhodesias indicates that another attempt is being made to force the issue for organic union of the Southern Rhodesia Christian Conference with the World Council of Churches.

a deep personal conviction that the time had arrived when the churches and missions at work in Southern Rhodesia should seek some form of church union, especially those churches and missions which were already akin to each other in polity.

He drew a parallel between the history of the early Church and the history of the churches in Southern Rhodesia, emphasizing that the early Church had no one polity. But experience taught that if it was to contend with its problems within and without, it must "seek a common mind on matters of discipline and doctrine." Therefore it was required of the Church in Southern Rhodesia "to put her house in order . . . and to seek a measure of common order."

The speaker thought that the absence of any marked desire so far for union was due to three reasons: (1) There was "no external force or enemy to drive us to the closing of our ranks." (2) There was "more than enough work to do in each of our areas." (3) The "stress and tension of the cost of any union," even between churches of the same denomination but of different lands, was more than we were prepared to face.

All "ecclesiastical marriages," he maintained, were fraught with hazards, yet it was imperative for us to do all we could "to foster union and to be obedient to our Lord's prayer 'that they all might be one.' "

Then as an illustration as to where missions or churches might begin uniting, the speaker [13] suggested an organic rapprochement between an Anabaptist oriented body, a Wesleyan-Arminian oriented body, and a Reformed-Calvinistic body, all of whom [14] he presumed had this common bond—they subscribed to the central authority of the Bible as the Word of God and had certain similar ethos patterns or ethi-

---

[13] The Reverend Fred B. Rea, Principal of the Epworth Theological College, Salisbury, Federation of Rhodesia and Nyasaland.

[14] The Brethren in Christ Church, The Free Methodist Church, and the Dutch Reformed Church of South Africa, respectively.

cal standards—and this in spite of the wide variance in church polity and theological perspectives.[15]

In other words, the issue must be forced regardless of the stress and strain and unnaturalness involved just for the sake of starting somewhere with *union,* which it was hoped would lead to *unity.*

2. *Biblical Unity*

The answer to all of this was given in a portion of the writer's presidential address at the same conference as follows:

> There is no doubt that consideration of the supraracial, supranational and supradenominational aspect of the Church will cause any thinking person to stop and ask himself the question, What did our Lord mean in His high-priestly prayer when He prayed, "That they all may be one; as thou, Father, art in me, . . . that the world may believe that thou hast sent me." Could it be that there has been a further unfortunate dichotomy between the mission of the Church and the unity of the Church? Undoubtedly there has.
>
> However, it is only fair to point out that notwithstanding the urgency to unity, in the words of Bishop Stephen Neill we must say,
>
>> "Now to affirm this urgency of mission is not to say that any or every kind of union is in itself good. Unity is to be sought not for the sake of unity but that the world may believe; and if at any point the choice is clearly between unity and truth, it is truth that must unhesitatingly be followed . . ."
>
> There are many of us in this Southern Rhodesia Christian Conference who recognize that unity can be achieved only in loyalty to Jesus Christ—the Christ of the Word, and to His Word—the Word of God. Within those loyal-

---

[15] Southern Rhodesia Christian Conference minutes, 1960, p. 21.

ties we are called today to deep heart-searchings and new efforts in expressing our oneness in Christ in our Church life. Such efforts will find ever-continuing expressions as the recent oneness and unity of the churches in the Billy Graham Crusade, with the result as reported in the April [1960] *Our Africa:*

"One young man told me that he had not been to church for a long time. But the sight of thousands and thousands of all races and backgrounds so impressed him that he said, 'This is the Church.' The oneness of the gathering brought to him the conviction that the Church is not in a building, but in a Body. Before the meeting was over he had given his heart to Jesus Christ." [16]

3. *The Larger Fellowship*

At that point it was the writer's view—and still is—that when it comes to any development in ecumenical patterns, we need to remember that the larger the fellowship we can achieve across the boundaries of our local circumstance, the more we will keep the interdenominational, the intercontinental and interchurch mission aspect in the life of our churches. For this reason some will continue to press for organic relationships with various groups representing varied theological and church interests. All should be prepared to recognize value where value may be obtained in uniting with international fellowships of churches, missions and similar federated interests. Where councils or conferences depart from their stated neutral position in ecumenical matters and consider the possibility of closer links with the World Council of Churches and such bodies as the All Africa Church Conference, they must also be prepared to recognize the validity of an organization of the World Evangelical Fellowship among interested churches. In the nar-

[16] *Ibid.*, pp. 16-17.

rower spheres of churchianity, they must also recognize the valid aspects of international affiliations of denominational groups.[17] For the World Council of Churches to oppose a world evangelical federation or an alliance of similar denominations is being terribly parochial. The WCC and allied national councils cannot oppose such affiliation in all good faith and hold to the *raison d'être* of their own being.

The conclusion to the consideration of interchurch cooperation, organization, alliance, and fellowship is most succinctly stated in a study in depth in which the writer participated but for which he does not claim personal authorship credit. He is quite prepared for it to stand by and large as his personal credo on the matter of principles of interchurch relationship:

> In view of the fact that it is the scriptural duty of all true Christians to relate to one another, we believe that we are to encourage fellowship for spiritual purposes among true believers in Christ. Spiritual fellowship can only be enjoyed by regenerated people whether as individuals or within organized groups.

4. *Fellowship and Cooperation*

Cooperation in our day is more commonly demonstrated within an organizational framework.

  a. Local secular matters, such as famine relief and government negotiations in areas of education, medicine, et cetera, sometimes necessitate joint action among mission societies and churches who may not be in complete agreement.

  b. On matters involving spiritual and theological issues, such as evangelism literature, et cetera, cooperation is to be sought only on the basis of agree-

---

[17] For example, the Anglican Communions, the World Lutheran Federation, the World Methodist Council, the World Baptist, and World Presbyterian Alliances, and the Mennonite World Conference affiliations.

ment on basic doctrines, especially the authority of the Scriptures. In the area of cooperation an orthodox doctrinal statement guarantees neither orthodoxy in the doctrine or life. The ease with which some liberals can sign orthodox doctrinal statements along with the failure of some conservative evangelicals to live up to the ethical implications of the things they profess to believe have greatly complicated the problem of cooperation.

Conservative evangelical church and mission leaders should educate their personnel, missionary and national, concerning the current theological issues and organizational trends that affect the Church. It should, however, be kept in mind that our main task is the spiritual one of evangelism and building up of the Church.

It is the writer's conviction that "existing evangelical fellowships should be strengthened for the purpose of achieving greater unity within our conservative evangelical ranks and to fulfill more effectively our evangelistic task."

He also feels that "careful consideration should be given to the possibility of establishing evangelical fellowships in countries where such do not now exist."

There are some existing evangelical fellowships and separate mission churches being approached by individuals representing organizations which are unsatisfactory, theologically, with a view to securing their participation and membership in such organizations. These approaches become more serious in view of the increasing desire of some national groups to relate themselves to other Christians throughout the world. Given such situations, we encourage national churches and missionaries to study the spiritual issues involved and to carefully consider the possibility of aligning themselves with conservative evangelical fellowships on a continental or international level.

Thus the answer in part to the critical problems of unity

and interchurch relations and participation today is found in Christians and evangelical churches getting together, in fellowship at the very least—a fellowship that crosses national and denominational boundaries. They should recognize the need for organic establishment of an alliance or fellowship of evangelical and theologically orthodox groups and churches on a supranational, supraracial, and supradenominational basis. Various existent groups and associations and fellowships should work together in harmony and even be drawn together so that the world evangelical Christian community may be one in the spirit of Christlike unity.

We do not want and neither do we need a world superchurch organization, but we desperately need a universal Christian fellowship that allows for differences within the common true faith. Thus we shall still foster interfellowship or associational relationship, and shall seek to live in spiritual fellowship with all Christian brethren; but we shall avoid any fatal compromise. So as to be continually relevant to the day in which we live, we need again and afresh to most carefully and most sensibly think through our Christian theology in the light of our evangelical heritage of scriptural and doctrinal understandings. Then we must act heroically as we are led by the Holy Spirit who will always help us to understand and accept the continuing basic Biblical principles in God's Word. In short, if we are truly Biblical and truly evangelical, we will associate with all those of like precious faith, we will not fight those with whom we do not fully see eye to eye, we will cooperate with all in those phases and programs where the name and Spirit of Christ may be honored. The Christian church and mission—yes, Christian survival— today more than ever demands this kind of appraisal and commitment.

❈   ❈   ❈   ❈   ❈   ❈   ❈

In this section we have attempted to discover answers to world missionary problems in the light of the Holy Scriptures. It is *one* thing to see what the Scripture teaches, and often *quite another* to put that teaching into practice. Our main concern here has been to give Biblical appraisal of world missions with emphasis on the situation and needs. We cannot stand aloof from the missionary cause and remain true Christians. We cannot observe missions in mortal danger without lending our hands, our heads, and our lives. Answers suggested here may not appear worthy to some readers. They are responsible to wrestle with these problems for themselves and to come up with some lines of action.

In conclusion, note what one leader writes of the Church: "She faces a radically new situation, and nothing will suffice save radical rethinking of the nature of her mission. Such rethinking must include both a realistic understanding of the new facts with which the mission has to deal, and a humble return to the source of the mission in the gospel. It must take both the Bible and the daily newspaper seriously. If it does, we can expect that the Church will be shown the new forms which must be taken for this new day by the mission which is the same from Christ's coming to His coming again." [18]

---

[18] Lesslie Newbigin, in foreword of *The Theology of the Christian Mission,* edited by Gerald H. Anderson (New York: McGraw-Hill Book Co., 1961), xiii.

CHAPTER IV

THE DIVINE AFFIRMATION

Noel Perkin

This gospel shall be preached—the end will come. "This gospel of the kingdom shall be preached in all the world for a witness unto all nations; and then shall the end come" (Matt. 24:14).

I. *The Immediate Need*

T HE QUESTION often asked is, Has the gospel been preached in all the world? Is the Church completed? Are there lands or areas where the gospel has not yet been preached?

It would be difficult at best to answer such questions with a positive and adequate reply, particularly when trying to determine the fulfillment of the Great Commission. To begin with, Jesus made it clear that such knowledge regarding God's program is unavailable when He said, "It is not for you to know the times or the seasons, which the Father hath put in his own power" (Acts 1:7).

Coupled with this statement, however, He added, "And ye shall be witnesses unto me . . . unto the uttermost part of the earth" (Acts 1:8).

With recent excursions into space and the speculations of scientists as to whether any of the planets are inhabited, we are at least certain that the Church's responsibility does not extend beyond the limits of the earth. The witness is unto the uttermost part of the earth.

130

A few years ago it was estimated by reliable authority that the only countries where there was no Christian church under national direction were Nepal, Afghanistan, Tibet, and Outer Mongolia. We know that the gospel has been carried into these countries at different times, but only God knows the degree to which Christ has been received.

The appeal today, in the recognized need for further evangelism, can be expressed more in unreached areas of life than by geographical boundaries.

The population of the world according to the most recent statistics provided by the United Nations is approximately three billion. The estimated Protestant church membership, and we must bear in mind that it is but an estimate, is 217 million or approximately 7 percent of the world population. This is according to the 1962 edition of the *Britannica Book of the Year.*

In *A Glimpse of World Missions* by Dr. Clyde W. Taylor, he states that the non-Christians in open mission fields number approximately 1,360,000,000.

These figures should be sufficient answer as to whether the task of witnessing has been completed. However, looking more closely at the areas of life still to be reached by the gospel, we might start with the primitive tribes who, because of diverse languages, difficulty of access, and hindering customs, have been largely neglected.

Dr. E. A. Nida of the American Bible Society stated in 1961 that "there are at least 1,000 tribes of people who have absolutely nothing of the Scriptures in their languages." This does not necessarily mean that the message has not been presented in some form orally to many of these tribes. It must also be kept in mind that many tribes may consist of only a few hundreds or thousands of people. The total number in all such tribes who do not have the Scriptures in their own language is estimated to be about 2 percent of the world's population. These unreached tribes are scattered in various parts of the world, primarily in Latin America,

Africa, and Southeast Asia. Naturally there is a strong appeal and romance in seeking to reach these needy people; but, as noted, they are by no means the largest group of unreached people as far as the gospel is concerned.

A tremendous segment of population is what might be described as the "poor" of this world. Protestantism as a whole has generally secured its adherents from what might be termed the middle class and perhaps the lower middle class, economically speaking. The very poor and completely illiterate in the main still present a strong appeal for evangelism. The masses of this class are still outside the reach and influence of the church.

World statistics in relation to population and groups are, at best, estimates. This is particularly true when we seek to determine the number of the "poor" which, of course, is a relative term. However, it may not be too far from the truth to state that one half of the world population is in this class. Poverty is further indicated by the fact that in 1959 it was estimated that at least seven hundred million people were illiterate and that half the world population rarely know what it means to have hunger completely satisfied.

The population of Red China is not common knowledge but, according to a 1962 United Nations report, it is 646 million. News reports (U. S. News and World Report, 1961) which are stated to come "from highly reliable sources, having access to the mass of information now flowing out of Red China," indicate an economic condition bordering on "disaster." It is this that caused Canada and Australia to send shipments of wheat. "A European engineer in one Chinese factory reports that 40 percent of the six thousand workers there were unable to work because of illness." It was further stated that "twenty to forty million Chinese were ordered back to the villages to grow food." In 1959 it was reported that the worst floods in one hundred years had come to China. These resulted in the loss of large parts of the rice crop, and some two million people were made homeless. The over-all picture in that great and heavily populated land cannot be described other than preponderately poor. If we should consider the smaller yet thickly populated area of India with its total of some four hundred and forty million, we again see the poor in the vast majority. It has been said that as many as a million people live on the streets of Calcutta with no place to rest except on the sidewalks. Be this as it may, while great strides have been taken to help alleviate the poverty and illiteracy of its people, India still needs help from outside its borders to meet its needs.

The great cities of the world with their slum areas are pivotal points from which flow every sort of evil influence. They call for concerted influence from evangelical churches throughout the world. It is stated that the cities comprise in their borders some 20 percent of the population of the world.

Dr. Wallace Merwin, quoting from a man in the Philippines, states, "The rich grow richer, but the poor grow poorer." He then adds, "The cities are changing, but the villages in the rural areas remain unchanged in their poverty. Behind the great concrete buildings of the cities are the hovels of the dispossessed, the poverty-stricken people of Asia. Ragged children poke in every garbage heap for something to eat, for something that can be used."

Compare the Protestant church membership in most of the large cities with the total population of the city, and it will be apparent that a great door is still open for further ministry. These cities represent the hub of life and activity in the respective areas and should have priority of consideration by missionary bodies. If we take the centers, the gospel will radiate to the surrounding areas.

To visualize the world picture in the broadest sense there is little danger of a challenge of facts if one states that the poor comprise at least 50 percent of the world population. More than 40 percent of these are as yet unreached by the gospel. Possibly the undenominational groups, the faith missions, and the Pentecostals are doing as much as any, and more than most, in bringing the gospel to this class.

Another class that is far from evangelized is the intelligentsia or the educated group. A high court judge in India when the British were still in authority was asked about his faith. He replied that he was reading the Bible more than any book and added, "The missionary does not approach us, I suppose because he thinks we do not want or need him." This man represents the hunger for truth that undoubtedly is in the hearts of many in the educated class who have not yet been confronted with the reality of the fact that Jesus lives. We cannot bring the world to Christ, but we can take Christ to the world.

There is a rapidly increasing interest in education. This is revealed in the United States by the fact that some twenty-five years ago there were only about 16 percent of high school graduates who sought to enter college while today 40 percent are applying for entrance. In the early twenties fewer than eight hundred thousand attended college in the U.S.A. Now there are about four million, and by 1975 it is expected there may be six million. In other lands, where a considerable degree of illiteracy prevails, it is estimated that some fifty million per year are learning to read. This is from the formerly illiterate class. Dr. Frank Laubach mentions in one of his books how small was the first response in the approach to the Moros of the Philippines when the gospel was presented. However, when an invitation was given to these same people to learn to read, thousands applied. The thirst for knowledge and the acquiring of it do not mean that the educated man, according to the standards of this world, is informed in the knowledge of God.

Nevertheless, this informed or educated class does present a great potential for leadership in evangelism if they become acquainted with Christ and possess that eternal life which comes from Him alone. Only those who are partakers of this life can witness of it to others.

The educated class, especially if we couple such with the wealthy, is distinctly in the minority and might be confined to as low as 5 percent of the world population.

We, therefore, find the unevangelized tribes, the poor of this world, as well as those who feel they are rich and increased with goods and knowledge but who are, nevertheless, poor and blind and naked. All of these present a challenge to the servants of Christ and call for a presentation of the gospel.

II. *Meeting the Need*

The purpose of witnessing is to impart life to the hearers. In Him was life, and to as many as received Him to them gave He power to become the sons of God. This process of giving life does not consist in merely repeating a formula such as "Believe on the Lord Jesus Christ, and thou shalt be saved." It may properly include this, but the hearer needs to understand what it means to believe in Christ. Christ must be so made known that He can be accepted, not as a figure of history, but as the One who is, and who is coming again to complete the triumph of redemption. In other words, it is not the accepting of a historical record or ecclesiastical formula but rather a yielding to a present living Christ who by His Spirit effects the salvation which His redeeming grace has made available.

This does not come through human wisdom or psychology. The woman at the well in Samaria could only see the physical and natural source of supply when Jesus said, "If thou knewest the gift of God, and who it is that saith to thee, Give me to drink; thou wouldest have asked of him, and he would have given thee living water." She, therefore, said, "Thou hast nothing to draw with, and the well is deep." The water of life comes from a source deeper and higher than any well of this world and does not require material means to reach it. Every true believer is a potential communicator of life to those whom he contacts from day to day. What we have received we must communicate to others if we are to have more. The law of the spiritual life is ever to "give, and it shall be given unto you." The fact that the church has largely left the communication of truth and the gospel to appointed leaders with resultant inactivity by the majority of believers is no doubt one basic cause of dissatisfaction in the hearts of many because of a lack of present blessing in the life. When we only receive and never give out, stagnation and unhappiness result.

The word of the Christian is primarily a witness of what he has known, felt, and experienced in Christ. Paul, who is set forth as an example to all believers, stated that he was called to be a witness both of things he had seen and of those things in which the Lord would yet appear unto him (Acts 26:16). This implied a progressive revelation of Christ which the believer receives as he daily presses on to know the Lord. What we thus receive must be shared with others, and then God adds more. The manifestation of the Spirit is not given primarily for our own personal profit, although it does bring this; but it is for the profit of all.

How many one finds who perpetually seek and implore God to bless them and pour His Spirit upon them who have failed to communicate to others what God has already given. The coming of the Spirit was first to make each member a witness.

One of the most serious deterrents to the fulfilling of God's purpose in the giving of the witness of Christ to the world is the indifference of so many of God's people, branches in the vine but without fruit. We are so occupied with our own business and make secondary or perhaps last the seeking of the kingdom of God which ought to be put at the top of the list. A church fully alive to our Father's business can accomplish our Lord's command to become a witness to all nations and all people.

The idea so prevalent in practice, if not in actual belief,

is that the preacher and missionary or professional evangelist
are the ones through whom converts are to be made and
through whom the gospel is to be spread. This, however, is
not the Bible order. The Scriptures state that He gave apostles, prophets, evangelists, pastors, and teachers "for the per-
fecting of the saints, for the work of the ministry." In other
words, the world will be evangelized by individual believers
who, as living cells or "lively stones," as the Scripture states,
being part of the divine body, produce other cells. Thus the
whole body grows and increases with the increase of God.
This is paralleled in the physical world, as in the growth of a
natural body there is a constant division of each living cell
into two, and the two become four and so on. Only the diseased cell ceases to increase itself in this manner. With what
incredible speed the world would hear the gospel if this
same measure of increase were duplicated in the spiritual
realm.

Paul in his letter to the Ephesians states, in regard to the
growth of the Church, that "the whole body fitly joined together and compacted by that which every joint supplieth
. . . maketh increase of the body." Again in Colossians 2:19
it is written, "Not holding the Head, from which all the body
by joints and bands having nourishment ministered . . .
increaseth with the increase of God."

The law of supply and demand has its counterpart in the
spiritual realm. An oversupply for which there is no outlet
surfeits the market. If we keep to ourselves what God has
done for us we hinder further inflow. Is this perhaps the
answer to much of the professed dryness in individual experience? The Spirit has been given not to make us happy,
though this inevitably results from His coming, nor to give
us power, as a personal satisfaction to us; but He comes to
perpetuate the ministry of Jesus that the witness to truth
and to God and to salvation may continue. Naturally, from
the Spirit's presence come the fruits of the Spirit which include joy and peace. These are, however, preceded by love

which inevitably expresses itself in self-giving. Repeating our question, How is the world need for evangelism to be met? We would answer, By every believer communicating to others what he has received. "Herein is my Father glorified, that ye bear much fruit" (John 15:8).

III. *The Message to Be Preached*

We are prone to emphasize the message of God as though directed alone to the individual. This, of course, is the strongest approach in that love of self is natural and when kept in proper relation to God and others is not wrong. Jesus said that the first and great commandment was to love God with all our heart, mind, and strength, and the second commandment was like unto it, "Thou shalt love thy neighbour as thyself." In other words, a proper regard for self is in God's order. We, therefore, emphasize that Christ died for our sins and was raised for our justification. It is apparent, however, that while God clearly reveals His interest in the individual, He is also interested in the world. He died for the world, and the "whole creation groaneth . . . waiting for the redemption of the body." The gospel that is to be preached is not only for the salvation of the individual soul but is the "gospel of the kingdom." It is apparent that the early disciples did not recognize the kingdom in its spiritual sense, for even after His resurrection the question on their lips was, "Wilt Thou at this time restore the kingdom?" To them it was a national and down-to-earth operation. The impression they evidently held from the Old Testament Scriptures was that the Messiah, whom they accepted Jesus to be, would reestablish a kingdom after the Davidic order in which Israel would be restored to a place of prominence and power among the nations.

Seemingly Jesus never defined the kingdom, although in the beginnirg of the Acts of the Apostles we are told that during the forty days after Christ's resurrection He was fre-

quently seen by His disciples, and at that time He spoke of
the things pertaining to His kingdom. Because of the revelation of the Scriptures, the kingdom of God lay within the
vocabulary of every Jew. It was something they understood
and longed for desperately. The kingdom, and all that term
includes, was evidently to the forefront in the thinking of
our Lord as He taught His disciples in that great prayer
which is probably repeated more often than any other and
yet actually prayed in faith too seldom: "Thy kingdom come.
Thy will be done in earth, as it is in heaven." That it is a
spiritual kingdom in one form is clear from the statement of
Jesus to Pilate when He said, "My kingdom is not of this
world." As such it is not established by human force but
through the revelation of Christ as Saviour and His acceptance as Lord. In its present spiritual form it constitutes the
Church over which He rules, the successor to Israel who
chose an earthly king. Christ must reign over the Church
today, but there is a day coming when the kingdom will be
established on this earth; then will He be King indeed, and
every knee shall bow before Him. Then will come the full
and most glorious vindication of the sufferings of our Lord
when every tongue shall confess that He is Lord, and the
kingdoms of this world will become the kingdoms of our
Lord. Unfortunately this does not mean that all hearts will
yield to Him even though every tongue will confess that He
is Lord. "The heart is deceitful above all things, and desperately wicked" (Jer. 17:9). God's true people are never
those who just bear the name, whether one claims to be a
descendant of Abraham, a citizen of Israel, or a Christian
church member. Only those who in heart have surrendered
to the Lordship of God and of His Christ are truly God's
people.

Our message, therefore, is that redemption has been accomplished, and God is appealing through His servants that
all men everywhere be reconciled to God. Now He stands at
the heart's door, but soon He will stand at the portals of this

world, and every eye shall see Him. We enter the kingdom now through the revelation and acceptance of Him who is Lord and Saviour. While God reigns in a sense over all the world throughout history, He reigns in a special way in His church which is His Body. There is a progressive development along so many lines. The kingdom of God is now, and it is yet to come. We have received God's salvation now, and there is before us a full revelation of that salvation which is yet to come. Christ has indeed come now to the hearts of believers, but He is yet to come in the fullness of power and glory. Now we know in part, but the time is coming when we shall know even as we are known.

Our message to the world could, therefore, be summarized in the words of Jesus when He said, "The time is fulfilled, and the kingdom of God is at hand: repent ye, and believe the gospel" (Mark 1:15).

IV. *Then Shall the End Come*

It is difficult for us to adjust our thinking to so radical a change as the sudden transition from a democracy to a government by the immediate direction of God, especially when we understand that this, in relation to the nations of this world, is to be instituted by a cataclysmic invasion from Heaven.

Of course, the term "the end" has a varying significance among the church denominations. To some it means the final judgment; to others it indicates the end of the world; but to many it means the end of the Church Age or the rapture of the Church.

The rapture of the Church is seemingly prior to the establishing of the kingdom of God on earth. Our Lord is evidently coming first at an unexpected time described as a "thief in the night" when "one is taken and another left" (I Thess. 4:16-5:2; Matt. 24:37-42).

On the other hand, the kingdom is established on earth by

a preliminary barrage of judgments too terrible for us to grasp in their full sense:

> And I saw heaven opened, and behold a white horse; and he that sat upon him was called Faithful and True, and in righteousness he doth judge and make war. . . . And the armies which were in heaven followed him. . . . And out of his mouth goeth a sharp sword, that with it he should smite the nations: and he shall rule them with a rod of iron: . . . And he hath on his vesture . . . a name written, KING OF KINGS AND LORD OF LORDS (Rev. 19:11-16).

Dr. John Bright in his book *The Kingdom of God* says:

> The missionary task of the Church is thus one of desperate importance. If the redemption of man awaits his faith in Christ and His kingdom, then to summon men to that faith is no fussy meddling; it is the pivotal activity of history. Indeed, it is possible to say that it is the only hope of mankind.